A Small House in Crete

This is the story of finding a small holiday home in a traditional Greek hill village and the subsequent joys and frustrations, in equal measure, of buying it by email.

The transition from regular holidaymakers to home owners is matched by a gradual immersion in Greek life with the change in perspective that this brings.

There is also the touchingly quick welcome as prospective residents by Greek friends and the introduction into some of the harsher realities of life in the locality. The sharing of the normal human worries the world over; of health, parenthood, business worries, road schemes and crime so often masked behind the welcoming smiles to the summer visitors.

The planning of the refurbishment is an exercise in the currently popular art of 'living small.' This is undertaken in a race of creativity with the eccentric architect who is one of life's worriers. The experience is enlivened by shifting local preservation rules and the need for details to be planned to the nth degree.

This must be done to ensure that modern living is at all possible in a very confined space that currently lacks all modern services apart from fresh air.

And it is all done from a distance of two thousand miles with infrequent visits and the further challenge of trying to learn a language with only half the letters recognised (and they have different sounds!) The enrolment into a Greek church school class where the other pupils are 4 to 12 year olds does little to build confidence – and don't even ask about the Christmas nativity play

Crete Home by Email

Dear Geoff,

Thank you for your email enquiry about our property list.

Prices for properties in that particular village are high and you may find more value for money in other villages.

When are you planning to come to Crete to see properties?

How is the weather in Sussex today? I hear it was very cold in the UK on the weekend. Yesterday here I was in shorts!

Kind regards.

H

Shorts in February !!- Not in Sussex – we were not planning immediately to travel to Crete again though we had holidayed there again the previous September as we had in the past eight years - so why Crete? Strangely, it all began in the mid-nineties when poor organisation together with some procrastination on my part found me in one of the local travel agents asking the dreaded question "well what have you got that is warm and available before the end of the school holidays" – (some four or five weeks later)

A list of suggestions was quickly and summarily dismissed – too English, too French, too expensive, too Spanish ......finally the suggestion – Crete – "it's a Greek island?" Some racking of my brain –could only dredge up the Minotaur and the labyrinth legend and some vague memory of a page of a war story in a late 50's early 60's Eagle comic – The battle for Crete –complete with shadowy pictures of German paratroopers arrived under cover of darkness– I concluded that our northern European EU cousins probably arrived there by less dramatic forms of transport now.

Crete, well yes –I'd better ring home to be sure it was ok – what the hell –it's two weeks time – I'll surprise them – so Crete it was!

The priorities for that first visit had been fairly simple –good weather, outdoor-living, good food –and drink, some entertainment for two teenage boys (but not too much entertainment) and really somewhere different.

We landed by night flight –but no parachutes – and being package
tourists spend too long in a coach and passing through some resorts
that appeared to meet my criteria of 'too much entertainment.' Thankfully, we eventually arrived at the town that still had some lights on
and some stragglers in the bars and restaurants around a small, pretty
harbour. The next morning by daylight the town was bustling but small
scale – the local people very friendly, the scenery was fantastic, so was
the weather, the local food was very fresh and the drink was cheap -
we have been returning ever since.

Dear Geoff,

Have you considered the attached property from our list ? It may be
over your budget but is totally ready to live in and would make a really
great holiday home.

You could also rent it out very easily to family and friends and make it
start paying for itself. With the older properties about which you were
making enquiries, they are going to need a lot of work (and money!)
and in same cases building permits for reparation work, whereas with
a ready apartment, you pay your money and that's it!

Please note that we can also assist in arranging mortgages via a bank.
If you think you would like to see this apartment and the other two
older properties, then shall we make an appointment to meet in the
town square at 10.00 a.m. on Thursday 5th?

Best wishes.

H

The Viewing

Hi again

Flying out tomorrow -I have not seen a reply but can still meet you for 10 on the 5/5 - shall we drive up to Pano and see you there ? My mobile is shown below

Geoff

The actual day arrived. We had been on the island for a couple of days and were now used to the bright sun, warm air and slower pace of life. We stood in the square near the clock tower and looked out for the agent. She arrived shortly after the agreed time and admitted that she had not heard from the vendor that morning and was a little confused about which house was for sale but she was sure that in true cretan style all would become clear and, for sure be ok!

Some ten minutes later the owner arrived and shook hands but seemed rather reticent and spoke in greek to the agent. We would be viewing two houses —one in Pano (higher) the other in Kato (lower)— the second one we believed was the one that we had seen the picture of on the web –it was in the budget we had allowed. The first was more mysterious, the agent had not seen it either ? Intriguing – we knew Pano having walked up there a few years before and had a drink at Maria's bar –a jolly lady who we chatted to in broken English and sign language at her kafenion - a few chairs outside her house with striking green and mediterranean blue paintwork.

We all got into the owners car which mysteriously was missing one rear passenger door handle and headed out of town in a cloud of dust – we hung on and eagerly anticipated what was in store. In minutes we entered the narrow alleys of Pano –some creative parking and the narrowness of the old streets meant the car was abandoned –we were led through the village past a mixture of ruined and renovated small stone houses. After walking below the church we recognised a familiar corner –Maria's bar – we turned down the hill, down some steps, first right, then left the alleyway now only wide enough for two people abreast and occasionally half blocked by an old wooden bench or a large pot of geraniums –the last turn into an alleyway with some of the path newly painted in dazzling white interspersed with stepping-stones in their natural yellows , browns and orange.

"Here" said the owner pointing to the right. Ahead there was a glimpse of the hills across the bay and a flash of turquoise of the distant bay. It was beautiful!

The house stood at the end of a short terrace, it's neighbour was brilliant white painted plaster with Mediterranean blue paintwork but this house was ancient yellowy-brown stones. The door was a faded brown wood, decorated with a black cross, the shutters upstairs were the faded blue green wood featured on Greek postcards and calendars –a colour not available in the shops – 'time faded blue green'- two metal bars stretched from the front walls across the alley to the house opposite –were they propping each other up ?

Was there a key?

The owner shrugged – the key was rusted in the keyhole in the door. I pushed the door open – inside in the gloom there was dry sweet smell – as my eyes became accustomed to the dark I realised that the reason I couldn't readily assess the scale of the room was the haystack that seemed to be the singular occupant of the room apart from a rough wooden staircase climbing out of it through a trap-door to up-stairs. Strange –this was bringing a whole new dimension to the term 'rustic' in the estate agents lexicon.

The hay stood at least four foot deep for much of downstairs –wading through it I cautiously tested the stairs –they were open tread rough wood and walking up them took me past a set of hanging strings with items that appeared to be only used by horses and donkeys as there was enough tack and bridles to fit out the coronation coach.

The main difficulty was the lack of light; all there was came from the open door and a small pocket torch. I tentatively tested the staircase and as I neared the top I was confronted with a large 'Ali Baba' clay pot –known as a pithori–almost as tall as me.

The rest of upstairs seemed full of other objects –their identity made all the more difficult by some ropes criss-crossing the room –draped with sacks ? There were other shapeless items including wooden rakes and other old implements –enough to furnish the average twee coun-try pub.

The shutters were difficult to open and the clutter on the floor made further investigation hazardous –plus what lived in the mountain of hay? I beat a retreat down the stairs.

Coming back outside into the bright light S. exchanged a glance with me – it meant this was just what we both had in mind. There was a small yard that had been painted and planted in the front of the house –up a few steps –we asked if this was included with the sale –it was, according to a brief conversation between the agent and the owner. This seemed strange, why was the house so original but the garden area restored ?

Taking a last look at the house we made our way back through the narrow village streets to the car for what was to prove, unbeknown to me at the time, one of the more frightening drives of my life- (and I include a memorable taxi ride in Naples!)

The four of us set off, initially on the village road, before we veered off through a gateway onto a cobbled track –this was a donkey track that we had previously walked but had never considered it suitable for vehicles!

The car careered down the roads –bouncing us around inside the small car – as the rough stone walls flashing past us –only inches either side of the car – I realised where the missing door handle had gone then, terrifyingly –we shot across the paved road and up the narrow alley into – with much relief –we staggered out of the car.

The second house was not what we were looking for, it lacked an outlook and was attached, rather alarmingly, to a more derelict building and sat rather forlornly in the shadow of the neighbouring buildings but it was in our price range and we had a feeling the first, more picturesque house would not be ! Could we see inside?

The strangest thing was the owner had no key for it and the gate to the small courtyard was locked with a chain and a large padlock. The owner via the agent said there was nothing to see inside anyway – strange.

As this property was the one we had seen on the website and was, to say the least, disappointing -the viewing ended rather flatly. Still we had the car trip back down the hill to the town square to look forward to!

Mercifully, perhaps sensing our growing disappointment, the owner drove more sedately and used the road rather than the cobbled footpath/donkey track. We arrived back in the square shaken but not stirred and rather reflective, again I asked the agent what the price was likely to be for the first house – she said the owner was unwilling to say at this stage. She had already said that she was thinking of increasing the price of the rather forlorn second house as the lack of interest suggested to her that it was priced too low !! My mind wandered back to some sixth form economics class decades ago where there was some unlikely explanation of "giffin" goods if I remember correctly, where sales were increased when the price was increased –something to do with potatoes in 18th century Ireland and the affordability of

meat. At last, first hand application of giffin goods –a pity that the cir-
cumstances where somewhat disappointing from a personal perspective.

The agent bade goodbye to the reticent owner who drove off in a cloud
of dust –leaving us to ponder. I suggested a cold drink and we sat at
the closest café in the square.

Over very welcome cold drinks I asked if this was usual to be selling a
house without a price and also to not allow potential buyers an internal
viewing.

It was explained that it was often the physically closest relative that
was 'put upon' by the rest of the family to manage the sale of a property within the family on their behalf and the reticence was an under-
standable reaction.

She would do her best to get a price and call us back but given that we
flew home the following Tuesday, only five days away, we were not optimistic.

We were told that we had the option of signing a power of attorney
with a local solicitor who could then complete the transaction locally,
on our behalf whilst we were back in the UK. This is a general power
that could be applied to this or any other transaction for a period of
one year from signing.

There was also discussion about the role of an architect and the need
for a building permit and payment of the local taxes it all sounded
pretty complex and I was trying to remember that we were not really
house hunting but having a holiday after a particularly stressful winter.

We tried to put the house to the back of our minds but that evening
we met our friends who were staying in a nearby village for drinks and
a meal and somehow ended up walking up the hill with them to see
the little house ! It met with their approval – particularly the position –
this was further reinforced by a trip to Marias bar. Her mezes dish this
evening was tomatoes and cheese with a take away cucumber should
you get peckish on the walk back down the hill !

As dusk fell we walked down the donkey track from Pano , no rally driven Fiats mercifully, then up to our favourite restaurant from which

you can look down to the harbour. It's a small restaurant under the vine leaves and stars – glorious fresh food, cheerfully served –and this would be the nearest restaurant to the little Pano house – a ten minute walk away ! Too good to be true. So we have to wait for the agent to hear from the owner who is clearly relying on sophisticated economic modelling for pricing purposes supplemented by unusual marketing strategies involving not showing the inside of any property for sale – this did not look like being easy.

The Concert

Next day we visited the weekly market in the town and drove away from the area for the day – driving up into the mountains to the Kathero plateau –seeing water in the river beds, usually dry later in the year.
This was early in the year for us – confirmed by seeing tadpoles – thousands and thousands of them –another first.

Late afternoon I returned to take another quick look at the house and took a few more photos –I couldn't resist it !
We needed something to take our minds off the wait for news of the house – the solution –local entertainment!

Since arriving on the island earlier in the week we had noticed posters publicising the event. Our lack of the greek language meant we had

not realised what was being advertised. The poster showed a carica-
ture of long haired biblical style figure with his eyes closed . On an
earlier visit we had been fortunate enough to collect two large posters
advertising an "Aquatic Circus" - the posters were everywhere and depicted scenes of drama worthy of Steven Spielberg. The style was mid-
50's comic book in garish colours with day-glo lettering for Aquatic Circus, underneath was some Italian writing describing the drama with a
pasted overlay for the date and venue in Greek. The first showed three
men in frogman, outfits, one piloting a midget submarine the others
wrestling a giant squid ! I am sure that BBC wildlife broadcasting had
told me only the previous year that a giant squid had never been cap-
tured alive so it had to be worth the ticket price !

The second poster was even more dramatic – it depicted a cavewoman
(think Racquel Welch –One million years BC) paddling in water with
piranhas and stalked from the bank by what appear to be spear carrying headhunters.

Finally, there was 'Metamorphoso " – the scariest of all, where a were-
wolf was shown morphing into another nubile beauty – we were never
able to obtain our own copy of this – we believe the circus was moving
around the island several days ahead giv-
ing local collectors the chance to take
them ahead of us.

Clearly, biblical man was relatively tame
but the posters seemed everywhere – we
needed to know more. The mystery was
solved a few days later when we saw notices in the town square for a concert at
the Community Hall that Friday –with
'biblical man'

Enquiries revealed that this was no mere
mortal but the world's greatest lyre play-
er and generally acknowledged to be a vir-
tuoso but also mysteriously described as 'fierce music.' We had to be
there.

We had been told by George that the concert, advertised as 10 p.m. would start late –this information was imparted as we asked for the bill at 9.50 knowing we had not received the normal free sweet or fruit course and raki licquor. We arrived ten minutes late – the hall was empty !

Outside the building and right on the seafront the town's cultural glitterati had gathered, talking, drinking and jingling worry beads and jewellery.

In one or two cases there was just some smoking and drinking whilst pacing in silent contemplation. We discovered later that some of the pacers were some of the star performers psyching themselves up for the performance. Tickets were 13 €uros each and appeared to be selling slowly although we discovered later that this cost was offset by a free drink from the bar. This was a makeshift affair on the counter of the information desk. Closer inspection revealed an impressive arsenal of spirits to be accompanied by nuts and biscuit nibbles, handily provided with large plastic dishes to ensure a good supply! The drinks – apparently spirits only – were dispensed in half pint glasses with ice with water and soft drinks only available 'under the counter' and somewhat begrudgingly. A request for wine or beer was dismissed – such drinks were considered too weedy for the time of day and strength of the music. We joined in the preparations with our halves of inspiration. The audience continued with their preparations on the terrace – the pace of drinking and smoking stepping up a gear.

At last – around 10.40 there was a gradual movement of people into the hall - most carried drinks The change of location and the brighter lights gave many the chance to embrace, shake hands and renew acquaintances with friends not spotted on the terrace.

The performers, five in all – with at least two moustache wearing heavies that had early been taken as taxi drivers ; a glamourous redhead goth lady and the maestro himself- biblical in appearance and resembling a refugee from a 70's prog rock band. Tuning up took place but not at such a volume to quell the mounting hubbub in the hall. A change of tactics was required and this was provided by the MC who provided a ten minute lecture on the musical feast in store –though this too failed to quieten the audience whose second or third large drinks were starting to kick in. Some of those who were less than en-grossed in proceedings and who could still stand up went to the bar to collect more alcoholic fuel before the proceedings started in earnest.

I was aware of a low droning which raised in pitch as the instruments were 'wound up' to cruising speed – the music was mesmorizing punc-tuated by the virtuoso's husky singing. I am not qualified to comment on the standard – but it was certainly different and some, (not all) of the local audience were enjoying it so much that they briefly stopped talking ! The full benefit of the performance was to some extent lost on us as we had no earlier lyre –based performance against which to compare. The music was interesting, quite hypnotic, unless that was the heavy duty spirits!

The wording seemed to be conveying some epic tale which was also lost on us. There was some change sound when the goth lady took over vocal duties and she had a clear strong voice contrasting with the gruff tone of the maestro. After almost an hour the lights went up and there was an exodus to the bar including the performers – we felt the burden of the week's excitement weighing heavily on our tired heads – we left for our bed.

Some News

Saturday we drove out into the mountains –stopping for a morning coffee in one of the larger mountain villages. Surprisingly we bumped into the agent on her way to her pilates class. There had been no word from the owners of the Pano house about the price – be patient, we would be sure to hear something before we left for home again – on Tuesday- four days away!

We tried to forget about the little house and drove on to Sitia for the afternoon, stopping for lunch in Mochlos on the coast where the fish restaurant veranda overlooked the archaeological excavations on the small island opposite and small boys fished in the sea.

That evening we met with our friends again who had returned from the far east of the island with tales of cheap houses – much better value than in this area but our hearts were set on the area and in truth, on the little house we had seen. Our friends pointed out that it couldn't be a serious sale otherwise the vendors would have instructed the agent and set a price! Reluctantly, we had to agree and tried to forget the house – not so easy as we returned to our favourite restaurant for supper.

The next day discussions with a friend confirmed our worst fears about Pano – unusual for anything to be sold up there, normally snapped up for prices at least double what we were budgeting. His bullish attitude was not helped in our eyes by the knowledge that his family had just finished building one of the larger houses in Pano – clearly it was in his interest to support that particular property micro-market. We could see the attraction though even as we braced ourselves for disappointment. The village was pretty had a few local bars and a shop and church. It was a short distance from the main town –steep but easily walked and because of the height gained possessed spectacular vies across the bay to the mountains beyond which at sunset we knew turned a candy pink !! Still no news on the price but it was Sunday and the day our friends returned to England. Yes, we would be sure to keep them up to date with developments on the house but we were becoming less hopeful by the day.

Monday morning saw us up early having a walk by the shore after gazing wistfully up at the village from the balcony of our rented apartment. The answer phone was on at the agents office and a call to her mobile brought no further news, we decided to drive out to Neapolis for some last minute shopping. There was a shop with original 50' and 60's patterned fabric that we had visited on our last trip.

On the way we passed another agent's office so out of frustration as much as anything else we called in. We were made welcome but their view of the local property market was not. New build was seen as the best option with building and ownership difficulties being major hurdles for old properties. There was also a view that anything decent particularly in town or immediate environs would be priced high due to the shortage of properties.

Our hearts fell so we made our excuses and left town for Neapolis. Once we were there our heart wasn't in it – we went for an iced coffee in the 30's style deco architecture hotel. Again we had a nice chat with the guy on the desk – in his impeccable English – the hotel was built in the 50's he told us and the business was a mix of tourists and local business. He told us more about the history of the town – we left the coolness of the hotel for the heat of the morning sun – commenting how we loved this island. Minutes later as we walked through the narrow streets my phone rang – it was agent –she had the price – the news was good –it was close to the price of the other small house - but there was some bad news – the little yard in front that had been painted was not included - that belonged to next door. Anyway think about it – and if we wanted to talk to her further she was in the office for the next hour and a half and was off that afternoon and evening but would be there tomorrow –the day we flew home to England.

Possibilities

It seemed a rush but what the hell – the house really seemed what we both had in our imagination, even before we had seen it and the price and location were right - we drove quickly to the town and with some difficulty found the architects office near the port. The office was reassuring framed plans and prints were on the wall –tidy shelves and drawers, interesting ornaments, an old art deco style bakelite radio, a row of buckets containing matching house plants – it reeked of style. We were briefly introduced to her colleague who looked after legal matters, planning and masterminded their company web-site. The architect himself smiled – he was just leaving the office carrying a stylish bulging leather brief-case –I secretly hoped it was his Alfa Romeo parked around the corner – it would complete the image.

We agreed that it was disappointing that the small yard was not part of the sale but this seem to be reflected in the price which we agreed seemed attractive. There had been time for her to have a brief discussion with her two colleagues and it was felt that a small balcony and a roof terrace was a possibility and would make up for the lack of outside space. It was also mentioned that a footpath in front was often used as a spot for a small table and a chair – there would be no cars – but maybe the odd cat or donkey.

Would there be any difficulty with a building permit ?

There was agreement that as the building was already a dwelling (albeit without water, drains, power, glass in the windows or a lock on the front door !) so there wasn't the hurdle of conversion to a house. (The fact that the sale was of a good position with spectacular views plus roof, walls and floor became a bit more worrying later when the survey revealed a wall crack, leaking roof and the floor would need excavating for the drains!)

Much of this, we realised was just skirting around the subject – it wasn't a question of economics –even greek economics. It would take years before the cost of the house would be offset by rental savings – but this wasn't a rational decision –it was about owning our own place in the sun –we had seen the TV programmes –read the travel books and magazines. What did we need to do next?

The agents were very cretan and low pressure – best to do nothing apart from appointing a solicitor with power of attorney –this could be done tomorrow morning. Then we should sleep on it, fly home – think about the transaction when back in England – then if we were still interested make an offer from there. They were not worried as they had a number of prospective buyers on their books who could be mailed later in the week if we decided not to go ahead and all we would have lost was a few hour and some 50 €uros for the power of attorney. An appointment was made to see a solicitor two roads away from the agent's office at ten o'clock tomorrow, some three and a half hours before we would drive away from the airport and back to springtime in England.

We drove back to the apartment in a daze – we needed lunch so we cleared the fridge in readiness for leaving for home the next day and put together a picnic and took it up to Pano –sitting near the church and admiring the view.
We wound our way through the alleyways from the church until we were again at the house – In the words of U2   the streets (and in our case –the houses) have no names.

We took some more photos and tried to see inside but couldn't easily open the shutters – so I shot off a few flash pictures hoping it might give us more of a clue to the interior and the mysterious contents. Reluctantly we started to leave but bumped into a tanned stranger – not Greek – but French –who turned out to be the proverbial man-next door. He smiled and seemed to be saying – in French – that the 'street' was a dead-end- but was happy to engage us in conversation –in french. Mine is rudimentary school boy 'o'-level scrape pass and rusty at that. I have usually taken the precaution of travelling in France in the company of some-one with a much better grasp of the language than me. Today I was alone – 'J'ai retiree' – he said – "moi –aussie" I replied – vaguely suspected that I may have told him I was Australian – he was from Paris and spent half the year here with his wife – we agreed the village was "tres jolie" as was his house –and the gladiolas –and his front door. We were very keen to leave – not just because this was my most vigorous French language work out for some years but there was a worry that he may not know "our house" as we were staring to think of the house we had been calling the "little house" was, in fact , for sale. From the paint work it looked like the small yard was his and "our house" was sandwiched between this and his house ! No we did not want to make him aware of it's availability – I was also considering future conversations –in French ? – about plans for a bal-cony or roof terrace –No, we needed to leave – now ! Our new best friend had other ideas – wasn't the view spectacular –there were oth-ers in the village who were not greeks – allemande, francais, Etais Unis – he waved to someone on a roof garden who called back – we made our excuses and left- with as much speed as our dignity allowed – he may be very wise –he said "au revoir"

I then explained that the previous week when she was having an af-ternoon nap and I had returned for a second look I had been hailed in French from their balcony where the same gentleman had been play-ing, I think backgammon or some other board game with madame. He had explained it was a dead end (cul-de-sac? though he disappointedly didn't say that)

I had pointed to my camera and mimed that I was photographing the view from the vantage point at the end of the alleyway where the view opened out. I hoped that the afternoon disguise of a different shirt sun glasses and panama hat threw him off the scent – anyway why would he want a hillside house in Crete – he already had one – and his probably had drains, water, glass in his windows – and I knew he had electricity, his meter was on the wall tantalisingly close to the front door of "our house"

Returning to town we called in the bookstore and gathered up some Greek and Italian home and design magazines and took them to a nearby beach to browse over a late afternoon drink.

No real escape there – a new clothes shop had opened – with beautiful sea green paintwork – but it was the small wooden balcony and the tiny spiral staircase that took our eye – it was as much as I could resist to avoid asking where they had come from –the builder's phone number and availabilities – we needed to return to the sanity of spring in England to think this through!

The Notary

Tuesday – our last day – up early – wistful gazing at Pano on the hill from our balcony again – where was the house? Photos taken to be scrutinised when we returned home. Our appointment with the notary was on this last morning in the next town – we drove there for nine-thirty at the architect's office to be taken to the notary's office for a ten o'clock appointment. Driving into sight of the harbour over the ridge a surreal sight met our eyes – a huge modern ocean liner dwarfing any of the high-rise hotels around the harbour. When we got nearer the real scale of this monster was apparent –towering above us from the roadside near the quay. The cabins boasted large patio doors and terraces – the ship bristled with satellite dishes and antennae and seemed to boast multiple helipads. It was "The World" and looked like it!

In true Cretan style to bring these nouveau riche down to earth the local agents had drawn the tiny 'Lotto' train alongside as transport into town where the cafes and restaurants could get the full benefit of these billionaires bank accounts. I had read about this leviathon and how you could cruise the world on board, effectively in your own apartment – a property paper had recently carried a multi million pound ad for a cabin.

It placed our own purchase in perspective – still our air- conditioned

Korean mini-car was more exclusive than the lotto train –"come on Bill (Gates?) move up and let Donald (Trump?) get a seat."

My daydream broken it was time to park and talk about this notary's appointment. The agents office looked bright and business like – yes they had seen the ship as well – monstrous! (and I guess not good for business if you arrive in your holiday home !)

With a little time to kill there was time to wet our appetites with some photos and plans of completed projects

It still all seemed a bit unreal. Did they really think something could be made of this little house – was a small balcony or a roof area a real option. "Certainly, these things were all possible once permits were obtained -the area was restricted development wise but these improvements should be permitted."

At 9.55 we were led around the corner and across two streets to the notary's office – up a staircase between a bakers and a shoe shop – to an empty office?? We waited but after only a short time a very business-like lady arrived dressed in a dark green tweedy suit, carrying a large leather briefcase and slightly out of breathe – the traffic –impossible, it used to be only 20 minutes from the courtroom in the neighbouring town – but now...Puff ! – impossible!

Well down to business, conducted partially in English but reverting not unreasonably to occasional greek with the agent. Did we have copies of our passports -yes this had been done at the agent's office. There was some hilarity over pronunciation – our parents names, professions and birthplaces were required – but difficulties were encountered not where we had expected –Llewellyn was handled with consummate ease as was Muriel – but Hertfordshire proved troublesome.

Then whilst we chatted with the agent about how the process had umpteen further options for potential derailment the notary entered the details into her pc.

After some ten minutes we were handed the power of attorney document – we recognised our names, addresses, professions, the details of our parents all sadly no longer with us – the rest was certainly all greek to us! Well, said the lady – we need two further copies –yes, I said. I was instructed that there was a copier some 3 or 4 doors down in a shop and for less than a euro they would provide the copies. Oh, I was meant to arrange this –fine... I set off and quickly located a stationers – who were happy to do the copying. I returned some minutes later realising I had seen some very smart if not commercially shrewd process re-engineering (as it's known to management consultants) This exercise with a UK solicitor would have cost plenty and taken some time – here – less than twenty minutes later and some £30 we had handed over our property purchasing rights to a solicitor we had yet to meet. Still on the way back we were shown her office –though it was acknowledged that she was not there today! She would be contacting us shortly –to send money if all went well!

We needed something to eat and drink.

Going Home

After saying goodbye to the agent and kissing each other on both cheeks – something I had not previously considered with an estate agent – we were wished luck and a safe journey home –Oh and don't forget to post copies of our birth certificates as soon as we were back home.

We collapsed into chairs outside the first café we saw – feeling exhausted and boggled – we ordered drinks and looked with bemusement at our greek document. This seemed a big step to be taking into the unknown –what were the costs of renovation? Would there be problems with building permits? Would the architect really take care of the project –could we manage this process from 2000 miles away? What was under that big pile of straw? Was there really no glass in the windows –and had anyone seen a drain?

Our faith in the possible was again restored when I went inside the café and asked for the bill and to use their bathroom – "you have got to see inside –it's like a designer hotel – gleaming curved bar, open tread glass stairs to a mezzanine and the bathroom- fabulous !" Well if we get this house - local style can do ancient or modern − and this was just in a café in the square, picked at random. They definitely do designer chic in Crete.

A quick stop in the grocers to take some local food delicacies home − rapid packing and cleaning the apartment − we were late. Goodbye's to Maria and a belated guilty admission about the house hunting − Where? Who are you buying it with? −Which agent? − relief −they are ok !

Rushing out of town −and late to the airport and the flight taking off early −unheard of. Four hours later our friends collecting us from Gatwick −

Good holiday − what did you buy − a house we think!!!!!
We are sleeping on it.

Back in Sussex in May it all seemed a little unreal: were we really doing this? We had agreed that we would go home and consider the house from England and if still interested we would submit an offer from home − a form of inverse high pressure salesmanship, cretan style. After 24 hours at home it still seemed a good idea, if a slightly scary one −it was so far away, needed so much work, so many unknowns but we loved the place −felt we knew it well, the people always made us welcome, it was an exciting new project at the right time for us and the price was accessible- though a moment of hesitation −what would it cost to restore?

We should have it surveyed but what if we lost it by hesitating −the seller seemed rather offhand and appeared to have little rapport with the agent.

It was decided rather rapidly, we would make an offer and then arrange a survey.

Emailing

We are safely back in the UK -sunny but cold here !

Thank you so much for your help yesterday and before

-we would like to proceed with the Pano property that we viewed with you last week.

Therefore, we wish to submit a formal offer at the proposed price.

We will copy our birth and marriage certificates and print the details and send these to you by post.

We would also like to proceed with the topographical/architectural survey

that we discussed in the office with you - will this include an opinion on the likelihood of gaining permission for a small balcony in the front upstairs , any option of a roof terrace and the option of a window opening in the front wall next to the door. I appreciate that details of this would be part of a larger piece of work for the necessary official building/repair approvals

Let us know what else we need to do at this stage

Thanks

Geoff and S

We now just had to wait whilst our hopes and dreams flashed through the internet. Never had switching on my Apple and opening email seemed so full of anticipation.

Dear Geoff and S
Sorry to hear about the cold weather. It is getting warmer here every day. We met with the vendors and I will get back to you tomorrow and confirm all your points.
Best wishes.
H

Dear Geoff and S
Further to your e-mail of 11 May, I confirm the price of the house in Pano and thank you for your formal offer.

Now you need to contact the lawyer, so send her an e-mail confirming this, informing her that you wish to proceed with the purchase of a house in , through us and that she has your power of attorney to proceed.
Please quote the reference number for the property and request her bank details in order to send the 10% deposit to block the property, the money for the search and any other amounts about which she instructs you.

In the meantime, you are posting to us copies of your birth certificates and marriage certificate.
If you would like a formal and written survey carried out on the property by the architect,
then the price of this is 250 Euros + 19% VAT.
Have a lovely weekend.

I had been given the business card of our solicitor who we had arranged power of attorney with but never met and had only seen her office on the way from the notary back to the agent's office on that hectic last day on the island. "You will remember it –the cheese shop is next door!"-they eat a lot of cheese in Crete – all that feta in greek salads –could I find it again –and more pressingly where was the business card? No matter, we would email and get the bank details –then send the money off to someone we had never met!

Dear Geoff & S
Thank you for your e-mail.
The Lawyer's e-mail address is shown below
For you to contact her.
Regarding the survey, you don't need to send the money with the deposit now. This can be done later on with the rest of the payments.
Enjoy your trip back at home and have a nice weekend.
Best wishes.
F.

Dear H and F
Hi
I hope you will have seen the correspondence with the lawyer which I am copying you in on. Hopefully things will proceed smoothly !!
We were wondering - as we had seen the Pano property before you had time to prepare them - whether you had any details that would give similar info
Such as approx size of rooms or even a small scale map of Pano and where it is there - We are probably being impatient and I guess this comes with the survey etc
Thanks again
Geoff and S
Ps we have now read the articles in the Greek Home magazine -we didn't notice before that it was by you and about the practice.

Dear Geoff and S
Yes, we are the famous stars of that magazine!
All the details you want will come with the survey.
Best wishes.

The Survey

Hi

We have received ok in the post today the birth certificates and the marriage certificates and will pass these on to the lawyer.

Best wishes.

H

Mr D

Sorry for not being able to inform you earlier about the transfer of your money due to our lot of work. I know that my secretary has already confirmed it to you, when you called her yesterday.

Thank you also for my fees.

I also wanted to inform you, that the legal survey is going to be completed

within 2 working days. I'll send you an email with the results on Wednesday morning if not earlier.

With my kindest regards,

L

Many thanks for the confirmation - we look forward to the results of the survey

Kindest regards

We have received written confirmation from our bank that the deposit was sent and I anticipated that it would be with your bank yesterday. Perhaps you would be kind enough to confirm that this is the case
Thanks you
Geoff and S

Survey Small Stone Gravity Construction -Pano

I am pleased to attach a copy of the survey with photographs, as carried out by the architect. Please confirm to me that you receive it ok and of course do not hesitate to let us know if you have any questions. Kind regards from a very warm and sunny Crete.
H

The survey made fascinating reading to us – it was well written in near-perfect English, well illustrated with photos some of which provided us with a better picture of the property than we had gained on those few visits a few weeks back. It also confirmed it actual metres what we were only too aware of already –it was tiny. It would need very careful planning to be able to use it –even for a holiday home but we always liked a challenge.

There was also some amusing references –the reason for these would be established later.

"On Small Stone Gravity Construction - (Stone built house)

Location: Pano village
Plot Area: 25.15 m2
House Area: 25.15 m2
Levels: Two (Ground floor and first floor)

This a two-level stone built house of an area of 25.15 m2, constructed on a plot of 25.15 m2, which means that it occupies all the plot area."

So this was confirmed –no garden but we knew that –we could still use the ground outside the front door to sit out on and we were planning a balcony and a roof terrace.

"Legal Aspects

The property house and plot exist prior to 1923.

It is certainly existing prior to 1985, which means that the plot is capable of accepting buildings according to the actual law. Pano village is defined as a traditional village and is regulated by the laws A.N. 2956/23/7/87 & ___845_/ 4/ 9/1987.

So, on the existing plot, in case the building was demolished, could build very little. But it can be maintained as it is and is fully legal, although it cannot accept any additions such as an extra floor."

Did this exclude a roof terrace ? We needed to find out –quickly -we had paid the deposit in a fit of optimism .

"Structural and Construction Aspects

The house is constructed in stone. The walls are thick 0,50 m. The connecting material used at the time of the house construction is not cement, but a mixture of soil and other natural material. This is the reason why afterwards it was pointed or plastered so that the consistency of the bearing walls is maintained keeping away water infiltrations which would harm it.
The foundations usually in these cases do not exist or are very shallow, but the Pano ground is extremely rocky which is positive."

Extremely rocky ground ! good job there is mains drainage and we don't have to have a septic tank dug or 'dynamited'

"The Wooden Floor

It is sound, made of pine wood beams and pine wood planks. Should you want to locate heavier materials, it would be better to reinforce it either with steel bars or extra beams."

So, some good news unless we are 'locating heavier materials' –given that upstairs had two large packing cases and 3 full sized oil drums, at least one of which I could not move it was hard to imagine what heavier materials we would be likely to locate –so probably good news then – and at least it probably meant the donkey hadn't ventured upstairs so that under the dust and hay there would be a lack of donkey dung! Good news I think.

"The Wooden Staircase With Hatch

This is sound although not very comfortable. In case you need to locate the vertical communication in a different way, you could have constructed a stone, other material, or anyway more comfortable wooden staircase."

Yes, more good news –the donk would not have attempted the stairs if they were uncomfortable – and no-one in their right mind would have tried to lead him up there – but on reflection did the house contents confirm a strong record of sanity –pass on that one for the moment.

"The Ceiling/Tiled Roof

This is rather rudimental. The beams are too distant from one another. There is no wooden plank part. It has no water or thermal insulation and it is visible that it is not water proof. It is covered with a French type tiles, the guttering is insufficient, old and not well located.

The Survey (part 2)

No doubt here – all bad news – and a new and not very pleasant sounding word –'rudimental' very apt – I have the photos – a lot in the house is rudimental!

"The Internal Plastering

In good quality except for one crack, probably due to water infiltration. Anyway during the phase of re-piping and re-cabling for plugs and switches and piping for plumbing, some of the plastering will be re-moved and then locally redone."
Bit mixed really – something of good quality –except for the crack

caused by a leak from the non-watertight roof and anyway some of

this good plaster will be removed – I guess the donkey sheltered

downstairs under the good floorboards and avoided the worst of the

infiltrations ! Don't blame him.

"Electric

"Was never electrified, but can be connected to the mains. "

Well a clean sheet of paper here.

Plumbing

"Was never connected to the mains but can be connected. Needs new plumbing."

Ditto – the non-existent plumbing can be connected once installed ?

"Cess Pit

It does not exist. Pano village is gradually being channeled to accept black waters which will be directed to the already constructed and op-erating central plant. There is not presently any sort of such a channel in front of the house and it seems that Pano is not going to be central-ly connected to the plant within the next five years. This means that it is necessary for the excavation of a cess pit to collect black waters and the only possible location of this is the ground flour area."

Not GOOD NEWS ! and I really don't want to think about it ! and the good rocky foundations definitely don't seem such good news now !!

"

Doors and Windows

These are very rudimental. The new ones have to be also in wood."

More rudimentals !! and the main thing is they are in the wrong place −not pointing at the spectacular view which is behind half a metre of stone !!

"Architectural Aspects and possible future actions

Without interfering externally – except for plastering – pointing - waterproofing - painting and after applying for a building permit, and obtaining it, the following actions could be done in order to make the house liveable.

Modernize, creating cess pit, plumbing and electric installation.

Change existing roof with flat roof, reinforcing all around top of walls applying chain in reinforced concrete.

Create wooden balcony where door/window is upstairs.

Create vertical communication up to future roof terrace.

Create kitchen corner and bathroom where most appropriate, according your needs and taste.

Well the creative bits sound good – although in the cold light of English day we are saying that we have paid a deposit on a house that has :-

- a leaky roof
- rudimental windows (in the wrong place)
- rudimental door
- uncomfortable stairs
- a first floor that will need re-inforcing if we are to locate heavier materials (that may include me and certainly includes some people I know!)
- no electrics
- no plumbing
- no drains
- walls that may need reinforcing if we are to get a roof terrace for a

view

So, we have bought a floor which we will need to dig up- through solid rock to arrange drains !

On the plus side, as S, the eternal optimist in all our projects – it is :-

- a very pretty house
- small to furnish and decorate
- in the right village
- with spectacular views (which I point out cannot be seen currently from anywhere in the house)
- we had already paid a several thousand euro deposit !

It was agreed, we would go ahead

Next Questions

H
Many thanks for this -it arrived OK -very interesting -I will draft our questions properly and send them and -if it's convenient also give you a call.

Just off the cuff I guess the first main questions that come to mind are :-

1. Is a balcony a definite option
2. Is a roof terrace a definite option
3. Is it normal and acceptable to site a cess- pit under the house -
if the house is only a holiday home will it require frequent emptying - if the ground is too rocky are there any alternative -what about 'gas outlets" ? Will this smell ?
4. For the suggested work - including a modest kitchen area and bathroom and use of normal (i.e. Not luxury fittings) could any indication of likely budget costings be given to include balcony, roof terrace and appropriate access.
I will put these out more fully tomorrow
Many thanks

Thank you for confirming receipt of the survey. In answer to your questions:
1) Is a balcony a definite option? Yes, proceeding towards a Building

Permit.

2) Is roof terrace a definite option? Yes, proceeding towards a Building Permit.

3) Regarding the cess pit, it is normal and acceptable in small villages and all new cess pits in the villages are done this way. The system done by the plumber afterwards has special piping for the cess pit and all the black water pipes, to an exhaust pipe on top of the roof. The cess pit inside is covered with reinforced concrete, which becomes the new floor of the room (obviously afterwards tiled) and has a cast iron double cover inspection box, which is sealed with grease.

4) If you can be more precise and give a more detailed list and specifications, then we can provide an approx. price.

Kind regards.

M - Architect

Thank you

What I was trying to do is establish a very rough estimate of a budget figure that we can use to establish what the potential costs are likely to be to take the small house from it's current state to a restored but modest holiday home.

As far as possible we would like to retain original features but appreciate to make the property secure and usable there are many things to do.

We are probably getting ahead of ourselves here as we are waiting for the results of the searches from the lawyer before we know that the property is free to purchase but once all is established as clear there and we ultimately take ownership we would very much like you to manage and execute the restoration project.

We do realise that this will require some detailed discussions on specification and consideration of options that your experience will be able to propose to us and would plan to do this by meeting with you in Crete.

Perhaps what I was asking was given your experience on similar projects in similar states and knowing the likely remedial work required would there be a range of estimates (probably only to nearest say 5,000 euros) that could be given as a yardstick for financial planning purposes to achieve the sort of remedial works described in the last paragraph of your survey?

For example I have no idea what it would cost to install a cess pit and reinstate the ground floor – similarly for the creation of a concrete roof and roof terrace. Please be assured that I would not in any way see the figure as any sort of quotation .

There seems nothing in your survey to suggest that it is uneconomic to restore the property and we are very much looking forward to doing this.

On one specific page 6 of the survey shows a picture described as Northern wall at ground floor – it is , I believe upstairs as there is no window in the northern wall on the ground floor – would it be permissable to install a window downstairs ?

Sorry if this goes on a bit and perhaps it is not possible to provide what I am hoping for and we will need to meet and talk things through at a later date
Thanks
Geoff

Estimates

Sorry for the huge delay in answering your questions, but I have been to Athens trying to sort out some health problems. I am back, everything seems ok regarding my health, and I will try to answer your questions.

The main problem is the material transportation and debris in and out, since the access is difficult. It is a common problem in our villages, but it makes it difficult to be precise on precosts since a lot has to be transported manually.

On the other hand the property is not extended and that is certainly keeping many costs low.

And everything of course depends on what exactly you want to do relating to specifications, qualities etc.

So,

*The Building Permit with related taxes and the IKA costs are approx. 7,500 Euros
'
*The cesspit excavation, debris removal, and new concrete floor could be approx. 4,500
Euros. This depends on how hard the rock is.

*Plumbing and electric could be approx. 5,000 Euros.

I think these are the most important expenses.

Regarding the opening of a window to downstairs of northern wall, this is requested with the building permit and is usually permitted.

I was anyway thinking that with the eastern wall overlooking the sea without windows, certainly windows cannot be put here through the building permit. But, if the owner of the bit of land in front, after discussing it, gives you the permission, then a small opening could be created, after him giving you his written authorization.

Kind regards.

E. Architect

Many thanks for the reply - we are pleased that you have resolved your health problem.

The answers to our questions are helpful and your office was also able to clarify some further issues when I phoned this morning.

Your suggestion of a small window to the east is a useful one and one that we should further explore.

In your survey you mentioned a small balcony and a roof terrace with suitable access and again these are matters we would wish to discuss further with you.

It seems that the best way forward is for us to be in further contact once the sale is finalised and to forward to you some matters for discussion where we would appreciate your professional consideration. These could be emailed to you then we could arrange a meeting with you when we come to Crete to properly discuss renovation options. We would also like to share some of ideas on taste and design with you so that we can understand each other. We are very impressed with the examples we have seen of past designs and projects.

We appreciate that this need not be rushed if we are to get to the best outcomes.

We are very excited about the project -we think the house is in a good location and the small size presents some opportunity for creative solutions as well as trying to gain the most from the location in terms of views etc

Thank you again

(I wanted to be sure that we remained on good terms with someone that was likely to be of vital importance to us and the house in the coming months so the emails were of necessity a little sycophantic- no matter.)

I am pleased to inform you that the papers from the vendor are nearly ready and the
notary has given me the costs for the contract. These are itemised on the attached schedule:

This must now be sent with the rest of purchase price, to the lawyer's account. Please do not forget to put reason for sending, "For the Purchase of a House in Crete", in order to avoid future tax problems. We also suggest sending a little more to cover bank costs. Any balance will of course be returned to you.

Kind regards.
F

Thanks for this -and it was useful discussing matters further with you. I am expecting the balance to be shown overleaf Say Hi to H
Thanks
Geoff

Dear Geoff,
Many greetings from here in a warm and sunny Crete. I am very pleased that everything seems to be progressing smoothly. E thanks you for your e-mail and agrees that it is much better to wait until the house sale has been completed and then get together to discuss the renovation.
We have also noted your other e-mail about the balance.
Hope you are both well.
H

Dear Geoff,
Thank you for arranging the transfer. No more is required. We will con-firm when it has arrived.

You made me laugh with the house insurance. It is always the first thing Brits ask about! I don't think the insurance company has any Greek customers, only foreigners! Anyway, that can be sorted out after the contract is signed, don't worry.

Glad the weather has improved. Enjoy the show in London.
Best wishes.
H

Dear Geoff,
The lawyer's office has just called us. The money is here!
Best wishes.

Strikes and Hospital

Further to our telephone conversation yesterday, I have spoken with the notary and the vendors have sorted out the papers with the one who is in hospital.

Monday is a public holiday here and on Tuesday the papers will go to the tax office and
the taxes will be paid, so the contract will be ready to be signed.
Best regards.
F
Who is in hospital – why –is it serious –was it a donkey related accident ?

Just to let you know that there will be a delay in signing of the contract as one of the vendors is still in hospital, so it will not be signed this week as hoped.
Will keep you informed.

Good morning from a very windy Crete.

44

I hope that both of you are fine there.

I have contacted the vendors and the Notary public regarding the papers for the completion.

They have an appointment on Friday with the Notary public in order to sign the necessary papers and bring them to the tax office. After that we need one or two working days for the contract to be signed when the taxes are paid.

For your information also, the banks are on strike more than two weeks now.

We hope to have everything finished by next wednesday.

We are sorry for any inconvenience but do know that this is an easy transaction

compare it to others that we have done that takes months of paperwork.

Best regards.

F

I hope that both of you are fine there.

All the papers for the contract are ready in the Tax Office and we are waiting from them confirmation to pay the taxes, get the receipt and sign the contract.

It seems that there is one person there taking care the papers for the sales so we have to be patient.

Best wishes from us here all.

Anxieties

The survey was completed today.
I confirm to you, that according to it, there are legal deeds of ownership of your vendor, copies of which you are going to receive at the
end of the
purchase's procedure. I also I confirm to you, that there are no legal
burdains, such as mortgages, claims etc and that the desired property
is appropriate for transfer.
According to the above I would like you to confirm to me, that I have
the right to pay off the deposit to the vendor this week from the money transfered to my bank account last week.
Also you'll be informed in coming days for the costs of the purchase,
so
that you can proceed to the transfer of them plus the rest of the
agreed
price.
Your tax numbers are also going to be issued on Friday by me.
For any questions that you may have, please feel free to contact me
any
time. I'll be glad to assist you.

With my kindest regards, T. solicitor

I'll proceed today to the pay off of the deposit.
We'll be in touch for the rest of the procedure.
Just have in mind, that I'll be out of office from 4th till 12th of June
Kind regards,
T

I would like to inform you that your remittance came yesterday to our
bank account.
Mrs T is going to contact with you next week.
With my kindest regards
Mrs T's secretary

Thanks for the confirmation
I rang your office this morning to find out about any progress and like-
ly dates for next steps.
We are hoping to come to Crete before a planned visit in september
and wanted to do that after we have possession of the Pano house
Best regards
Geoff

Thank you for your quick reply.
I estimate, that the exchange of contracts will be done sometime next
week. Of course, you'll be informed by our office about the precise
date of the contracts' signatures.
With my kindest regards,
Mrs T's secretary

Mrs T
Thanks you for your reassurances – I guess we just get a little anxious
as it seems so far away in distance.
Please advise us as soon as you know the sign over arrangements as it
is now almost two weeks since we transferred the funds for purchase

on the 8/6 in the UK.
Let us hope we hear about completion soon
Best regards

Thank you for your quick reply.
I estimate, that the exchange of contracts will be done sometime next week. Of course, you'll be informed by our office about the precise date of the contracts' signatures.
With my kindest regards,
Mrs T's secretary

H and F
We have the opportunity to come out again at the end of the month on 26/7 for a week. Before I book anything I wonder if you can tell me if you currently believe that the transaction will be finalised before that date -(I realise there may be some guesswork involved)
Otherwise the next time we can come will be in September.
Thanks

Ps Hot in England at the moment - but a bit strange -I was in London last Thursday when the bombs went off - not good

At Last –the Key to the Door!

Thank you very much for your email.
The contract is going to be signed the coming week, since the vendors
are going to settle their final obligations to the tax office regarding this
sale, hoping that the banks' strike will finally come to its end.I know
that
you worry, but I just want to pay your attention to the fact, that sometimes there are factors that is not up to us (unfortunately).
So you'll hear from me the day before the signature!
Kind regards,
T. Solicitor

Thank you very much
The agent had also kindly passed us similar information – we look forward to next week and owning our own little holiday home in Crete

I hope that both of you are fine there.
All the papers for the contract are ready in the Tax Office and we are
waiting from them
confirmation to pay the taxes, get the receipt and sign the contract.
It seems that there is one person there taking care the papers for the
sales so we have
to be patient.
Best wishes from us here all.
F

Thanks for the information -glad to hear the bank strike is over
Look forward to further news in due course

CONGRATULATIONS!!! The contract for the house has finally been
signed. You are now the proud owners of a property in Crete.
Yes, do please book your holiday for 26 July, but it may not be possible
to discuss the renovation work with you due to holiday commitments.
However, you can spend time at the house and formulate your ideas.
Many best wishes from all of us.
F

That is great news -thank you so much for all your help -
We will ring you soon - and we will arrange an early visit
We are VERY EXCITED !!! we love Crete so much ..

We have now booked flights for the night of 26th arriving in Crete early on 27th for one week -we look forward to meeting with you again

As you were already informed you are now the
owners of the desired house.
The contract was finally signed yesterday. Congratulations!
Because you are going to come this month I'll be
glad to set up an appointment with you and deliver you the documents
and the balance.
Kind regards,
T

It was really ours –The little house ! We could now call it our house !
what had we done ?

Stealth Motorbikes at Dawn

We arrived back at the end of July, by night. The airport car park was still hot with a heady mix of smells combining aviation fuel with the tamarisk and bougainvillea. The car hire security worked – the usual whispered instructions only days before –"the keys will be under the driver's floor-mat, the car unlocked – ring the day before and I will give you the colour and number of the plate; you don't want to drive the wrong car here" – the whole car park was probably filled with un-locked cars –all with the keys under the driver's mat – we were back in Crete and it was great to be here !

Minutes later as we drove towards the sunrise we encountered our first hazard – a stealth motorcyclist ! Hunched over his handlebars and in the middle of our side of the road –no apparent rear lights and a bare-ly discernible dim glow in the front. The road was windy and the tradi-tional method of overtaking is to tailgate until the vehicle in front pan-ics and pulls over to drive on the hard shoulder trusting there are no parked cars, pedestrians, fruit stall or large rocks –all of which we have encountered at one time or another when becoming forcibly en-

51

gaged in such manoeuvres. He was travelling at 70 kph plus but the road was pretty quiet – was it better to have him behind me or in front. Of course, if I rear-ended him his obvious defence would be that he had lights before I drove into him- cunning, or what. Was he drunk, mad or both ? Eventually we got past him and spent the next few miles worrying about him overtaking under cover of darkness until we concluded he had turned or fallen off. We drove as the sun rose –like a Texan road movie with mountains and scree slopes slipping past – eventually stopping in Agios for an essential six o'clock coffee and cheese pie in a street-side café – the temperature was in the high twenties and rising rapidly.

It was hard to believe but as we drove towards the town and Maria's apartment that we stayed in that we now owned a house on this is-land!! We had booked a night flight and even after the coffee we were still sleepy. Despite the excitement we would try and sleep – it was not a success so around an hour and a half later we were driving up the hill to the old village and our house!
Parking above the town behind the larger of the churches we walked through the narrow alleys of the village. The morning was already hot with deep shadows cast across the stone walkways, cats running at the sound of our feet. We saw no-one and turned the last corner be-fore our house and down into our tiny street.
The house was as we had left it some three months before with two notable exceptions –the climbing vines up the wall were even higher and the made the narrow alley even greener than before –secondly, there was a small mountain of black plastic sacks stacked against the front wall and virtually blocking the end of the alley. This was also blocking the access to their small courtyard for our neighbour –not a good start.
We went in – well half the hay had been bagged up but there was still a lot in there plus the large collection of pointy sticks and the much coveted clay urn. So good and bad news. We clambered over the de-bris and up the wooden staircase, through the hatch to admire the view from upstairs. Unfortunately, upstairs looked the same as at the last visit, a large wooden crate draped with sacks, several washing lines with more sacks and some mysterious plastic bottles tied to the line. Three large oil drums, one with a cover, two square tins, the urn and a large bowl completed the treasury- oh, and a small sprinkling of

hay (as if we didn't already have enough downstairs) All of this was now made more visible as the wooden shutters that had covered the windows had been thrown widely open by whoever had started to clear the house.

The Local

We needed to sit down and consider the position. Luckily, we had brought a celebratory bottle of sparkling and some grapes –we made the two square feta tins marginally more comfortable with sackcloth upholstery and sat precariously in the larger of the two windows – where we had optimistically discussed adding a small balcony with the architect. From here, if we risked our necks by leaning out we had a spectacular view of the causeway and the distant mountains across the lagoon. The view was slightly soured by the twenty or thirty or so plastic sacks rather more immediately in our view. The wine and grapes softened the prospect as we toasted our new little home.

But what would we do about the newly acquired contents and what was happening about them? We needed to find out and as potential new village residents we went to the place that all villagers go to find things out –the kafenion. Maria's was the only one we had visited before and although hardly regulars we felt sure of a warm welcome and we were not disappointed.

We had a pre-prepared short speech in greek to explain we had bought a small house in Pano Elounda and once renovated would be more frequent visitors. Maria seemed a little foxed by this and showing the photo didn't seem to clear things up, in fact she didn't seem to recognise the house which was less than a hundred yards away. Disappointed we settled down to our drinks and she plied us with mezes – three separate tiny courses – a salad of feta cheese, cucumber and tomatoes, water melon pieces and finally small fresh figs – 4 euros to include two beers. Yes, this was our local even if Maria had yet to realise it. We would return with help !

After a sleep we hit town for sundowners and dinner ! Also to update friends on progress since the visit in May. We first encountered Stelios and Costos outside his shop and two doors down from the jewellers where Costos delicately practised his art of jewellery making. This seems quite plausible on first meeting him – a delicate, lively man with bright eyes. Until that is you learnt more about his lifestyle which is more centred on bikes, heavy metal music and allegedly shooting anything that moves. Our recent acquisition on the Pano house was met with approval and even the threat of Costos becoming a neighbour at some indeterminate point in the future when he thinks he might live nearer the hills –handy for hunting! We mentioned the unmoved hay – and there was some sympathy and an immediate offer of markmanship to shoot anything that may lurk within –"cats, rats, mice – the trouble with you English is that you feed animals –then you have hundreds –shooting is the answer-let me know if there is anything you want shooting !!" Could be handy if there were any future disputes with neighbours or builders –though come to think of it they may be armed to the teeth as well- best not to start this arms race. We thanked them hoped the hired gun offer was in jest and went for a drink.

More advice – this time from George's Danish girlfriend – don't come here all the time like some others –unless you get a job –you will be bored. We explained that it was only a very small house, it could only be a holiday home ... that was alright then. There was then mention that they may also become neighbours –George owned some land near Pano – maybe they would build a house up there, it's very quiet – tranquil even – toasts to that –drinks on the house –see you later for a nightcap or later in the week if too tired all offers of payment were waved aside – we may be neighbours –(hopefully, not sheltering together from the trigger happy Costos and his one man vermin extermination squad-shattering the tranquillity.)

Time to eat – the first restaurant we came to was one we knew well where George, looking rather racy in an orange silk shirt greeted us with enthusiasm and a not altogether welcome patting of my stomach accompanied by the dubious compliment of "still sexy!" – was gay pride returning to Greece ?" – reassuringly his more refined wife also welcomed us for what was our first of many enjoyable meals that week. As we paid the bill some two hours later we resisted the tempting – how about another carafe for the road –on the house –these people know an awful lot about hospitality – nevertheless we declined and crawled up the hill to bed –we faced a busy week.

A late start after yesterday's travel and excitement – a good job we had resisted the carafe for the road. S. walked down to the bakers for some fresh bread –the English holiday cliché but always a good start to the day. Breakfast on the balcony – bread and olive paste, cheese and fruit – healthy. Maria said we could meet her in the square –she would drive down the hill then have the car there to collect shopping later. We drove down the hill –always exciting as the roads to down are single file only and additional hazards of cats, ladies sitting on roadside benches as well as oncoming cars or motorbikes. We arrived in the square without incident and realised the arrangements with Maria had been rather imprecise –in the square -in ten minutes. We hung around near the harbour which I defined as the square and at least there was something to watch- eventually Maria appeared –I had trouble parking and then started talking... we guessed as much-that was all part of the charm of the place –it was impossible for us to pass through town without a couple of conversations – for locals whole days could drift by!

We all got in the hire car and headed up the hill to Pano –Maria adding an element of unnecessary drama to the journey by refusing to wear a seat belt and carrying out her own elaborate hand signals in the front to help punctuate the conversation –"park here –it's nearer" assisted by vigorous hand signals –leaving me with only light bruises. We parked and were instructed by Maria how we must leave the car locked with the windows half open ? For years we had given up locking our hire cars as no-one else seemed to – and were quite happy to leave shopping in it – a pleasant change –and our greek friends found it hard to believe it was recommended to lock your car in a filling station in Britain whilst going to pay – although they conceded it was the same in Athens.

Progress through the village was slower with Maria – the people we had exchanged a kalimera or Yas or just a smile -were the opportunity for longer and animated conversation for Maria –including pointing to-wards us as part of the conversation – (I was hoping it wasn't all greek for "these are the mugs who have paid for Dimitri's new BMW by buy-ing his donkey shelter!!")

Every time we came up here we were charmed by the winding, narrow alleys, the kaleidoscope of colours on the walls of the little houses, the noises and smells. We turned down the last alley – the black sacks had multiplied – twice as many as yesterday- we clambered past them – both chattering to Maria – it's very small but it's what we want –and it's dry and we'll be getting more windows to get more light in and the architect says it's solid and he can really make something of it!! And and ……. Maria looked around and to our relief agreed –"yes –it's a good house, a good position, you will be able to make something of this –let's see upstairs"

With the additional hay clearance that had taken place upstairs was now much more chaotic than the ground floor.

57

"See there is this big urn and an earthenware bowl, and a niche over there –you can get sea view from the windows and this big one would be the door to the balcony if we get the building permit ...." We were like garrulous children – we desperately wanted her to like it – the same as months earlier even before we had known the price or made an offer but were already feeling unrealistically possessive we had shown the house to friends Dave and Miranda.

In the conversation we had ignored the other fittings the house came with –the three full sized oil drums, the two large wooden boxes, the old washing lines with their interesting collection of dusty sacks pegged to them as well as the superb collection of hand-carved pointy sticks !!

Going outside it was difficult to convince Maria that the small courtyard down the alley and next to our house was not ours but instead belonged to next door –it admittedly seemed strange in that our house was between the courtyard and the neighbours house but we explained that the lawyer had completed the land searches etc and confirmed that the little house came without outside space so apart from the shared common-way of the alley in front the only opportunity for outside space was a balcony and a roof terrace –both subject to building permits. I could see Maria was not entirely convinced. We left the house suggesting a drink at the nearest Kafenion, coincidentally owned by another Maria.

Maria speaks to Maria

En route we encountered a smiling elderly lady who Maria engaged in conversation which went on for ages with much pointing at the little house and at us. I am still not sure how much of the conversation was diplomatically edited for us but the upshot was that Maria −on the basis of this conversation with a neighbour now accepted that the small courtyard belonged to our neighbour −from what we could see -currently the only other occupied house in the street −the other two looking even more derelict than ours. Obviously, that is the answer − move into the street first and buy any spare areas. It appears, as Maria explained later that the next-door neighbours bought their house from the same family who had owned our house, as well as the small courtyard. So mystery solved. This was explained over drinks at Maria's kafenion where Maria 1 cleared up any confusion that Maria 2 may have suffered as a result of our experiments in the greek language. We think Maria 2 now understood we were to become neighbours. More mezes were brought out so that seemed ok.

Maria 1 was anxious that we came with her to meet an english family who had restored a house nearby − we finished our drinks but could not leave as unbeknown to us in one of the verbal exchanges in rapid greek Maria 2 had entrusted the bar to Maria 1 − no matter that we were the only customers −we could not leave until she returned. This

59

happened fairly soon –the urgent horn hooting we had noticed earlier had signalled the arrival of the bread van in the village and Maria had now returned armed with bags of rolls and loaves – perhaps a rush of the greek equivalent of ploughman's lunches were predicted. We paid and left promising to return soon –well it would be our local and I had never been asked to look after a pub in Sussex in the 20 years I had lived there!

In retrospect I realise Maria was only looking out for our interests as strangers in a foreign land – I suppose it was a good thing the neighbour agreed with the lawyer, estate agent and the greek land registry! We called in to see some friends of Marias who had renovated a larger house not 100 yards from the kafenion, did they know our little house –no they couldn't place it...the village is a real rabbit warren but very friendly. They showed us around their house which looked very comfortable and finished – a complete lack of hay –wonder if they need any –they are local – I could deliver.

On their terrace a lady who ran the restaurant was having a drink with their daughter –we exchanged 'hellos' - small world –you are buying – good –we will see more of you at the restaurant –it was always busy there and we realised this was the first time we had ever seen her sitting down!

On the way back to town Maria recounted some more of the conversation with the lady in black – yes the neighbour's house and ours had been owned by the same family and indeed ours had in recent times been used for stabling and storage –though the lady was new to the village and could only talk about the last twenty years. The owner is building a bar on the road south out of town –she has two sons but the house is not being cleared by them –she has two Albanians doing this ! She owned the house together with her brother (the one with the moustache) and her aunt. A wealth of information had been acquired – Albanians were playing a part in my life for the first time – even though I had not met them. We had also been involved in a transaction with someone whose main claim to fame was his moustache! In the land of moustaches we would see this guy coming – I had fantasies of following him on a motorbike, moustache billowing in the slipstream- perhaps obscuring his rear light and explaining a mystery earlier in the week.

The journey back to town was not without event – Maria suddenly ex-claimed "there's a van !" I braked hard and nearly sent her through the windscreen as she had still resisted the temptations of the seat belt. I assumed she had spotted a hazard on the road ahead- but she was merely updating us on the retail facilities available in the village and explaining where Maria 2 had obtained her bags of bread.

Back in town we ate a leisurely lunch of local traditional fare including horta – the local dish a mixture of boiled greens –almost like spinach with small asparagus type plants in it. I speculated whether the hay had been horta when first stored and if the Albanians had moved more swiftly could they have pioneered the Med's fast food veggie horta business –an opportunity missed, maybe.

Slowly, slowly and quickly, quickly.

"Quickly, quickly – it may seem mad but you must come with me –
you must come now –follow me! "
We followed the Architect out of the office and into the street. He
dashed up some steps and into a small tunnel like building that we
were told was a Byzantian church, rarely open but being cleaned by
two ladies – one of whom he had apparently spotted in the street,
hence the rush. There was some casual discussion of the architecture
and the restored frescos and then the conversation changed –"are you
cold?" - "no", I replied –"but this is a stone building too – with small
windows also" –"You must have air-conditioning in the Pano house" –
back to the office then !
I think I understood the reason for the visit – it had certainly taken a
short-cut through the discussion on heating.
Some two hours before we had renewed our acquaintance with the Architect which to date had been developing by email and phone. We
had shaken hands in May as he passed us in the office but we were
only buyers then now we would be involved together in the more serious and intricate process of renovation. We had arrived too early for a
six thirty appointment that I had mistakenly thought was for six
o'clock. It was agreed we would go off for a welcome cold drink, it was
still near thirty degrees even in the early evening and we rehearsed
the sort of areas we wanted to discuss. A small photo portfolio of

62

things we liked and projects we had completed at home had been brought along in the hope of speeding the designer/client ` getting to know us process.'

We were unsure whether this was the right thing but it felt like it and the décor and design of his office had already made us feel that they were our sort of folk. Clean designs and photo layouts were mixed with old radios and stereos, books, journals, stylish furniture and painted sticks and stones in rows of galvanised bucket planters.

We need not have worried –the portfolio of inspirations pictures was a success and the Architect himself, a bright eyed owl of a man became more and more animated and amused by these vignettes of our life – "and this caravan is in your garden?" – these coloured cupboards- these are in your kitchen –they are school lockers –bravo – yes I can see you like colour. This is helpful- look at this – a mad little van – yes a VW."

His estate agent had joined us and there was the opportunity to thanks him for steering us through the buying process, which I freely admitted had been a little worrying at times from the distance of two thousand miles.

"Coffee or cold drinks – let me show you some of our work "

There followed one of the most interesting hours I could ever remember spending – certainly in anyone's office, as we were guided through photos their PC of recent and past projects both new-build and renovations. The pictures showed bold modern edifices of white concrete and plate glass as well as old stone converted olive presses and windmills. But our house is very small, can interesting things still be done? –"Of course, because it is small interesting things must be done!"

There were details of windows and doors, limestone floors and pastel painted woodwork, beautiful lights and fittings – it was all truly inspired –we had found a serious architect here – and an artist who was clearly proud of his craft.

There will be much to discuss –much to plan in the house –where to put things –the specification of fittings –what could be re-used –so much to consider-exciting yes?

It was suggested that it would be necessary to prepare drawings in a lot of detail to get agreement on precise specification and we agreed that it seemed especially important given the space restrictions and the other requirements – Pano is in effect a 'listed village' so proposals need to be sympathetic and take into consideration what would be acceptable- but his humour broke through – "it does not mean the design should be safe and boring, it is a holiday home and holidays should be fun, yes!"

The drawings would contain details of electrics, door furniture, plumbing, air-conditioning –"wait a mo" –my northern European roots revealed themselves-"is air-conditioning strictly necessary" – "you want to be comfortable-this is Crete-it is essential" –

"but this is an old stone house-built on rock-with small windows- half metre thick stone walls, shutters -surely it will be cool even in summer?" The conversation moved on –I felt my protestations may have been ignored –no matter it was early days –and it was fascinating listening to a master enthusing about the possible and being so positive – many requests were met with "of course –that could be done" or " we could certainly look at doing that"

There was none of the teeth sucking and tutting and muttering that seemed to characterise the British building industry – this seemed to be Mediterranean creativity at it's best. Even corrections were handled with charm and sublety – after and hour and an a half the previously related drama unfolded as we were given our 'air conditioning lesson' But there was no crowing over a victory and upon returning to the office the conversation became more playful – your 'inspirations ' show you understand elements of living in small spaces – you need to be able to convert things – a table becomes a shelf- the loft hatch becomes the floor again –there must be versatility – a washing machine becomes a bed – we all threw in more and more absurd suggestions. We had so much food for thought – but were reassured by the parting comment – "there is much that can be done – it is a good house a –a good space. You have seen pictures and plans – come with me to see some buildings" – we were hoping for this offer since it had been casually mentioned during earlier conversations-"Yes, that would be really helpful-great –when?"

"Tomorrow – meet me here at ten thirty- come with me on some site visits"

"Yes, please –great-thanks"

"ok- we will meet again tomorrow"

Arriving at the office for 10.30 and after a quick, cold drink we were off to the hills in the company four-wheel drive. En route some natural history lessons of the island were relayed to us concerning olive tree planting and the use of the carob tree –which include photographic processing!

Fairly soon we arrived in a hill town of where he had a site visit which we would accompany him on. But first of all we drove through the narrow streets on the southern outskirts of the town climbing up through the town to park behind a church with spectacular views. Opposite the church he pointed out an interesting stone building with a walled garden and rich honey coloured windows and doors. It was an old olive press building and outhouses which had been sympathetically converted to a modernised home. The newly pointed mortar between the old stones were drawn to our attention –"this will be necessary in your house-if it is to keep out the water" –well we need that –the water we need is not that sort but mains water –another something to be arranged. We also noticed a strange pattern to one of the lintels over a small side window –it looked like a wooden turned screw some five foot long. "Yes that is interesting, it is part of the old mill mechanism that has been recovered to make the lintel and connect with the building's original purpose." A nice decorative and sensitive touch – very typical of his style we were to discover

We drove further up the hill to park again and this time we followed him into a town house with a wrought iron balcony. As soon as we

65

were inside we could see this was a finished project – the interior was newly painted white with a pistachio green finish to the woodwork –the whole impression was all very cool and clean. The first room was white and cool with a tiled wet room behind a sliding glass frame then stairs led up to a first floor room with pale green stained floorboards and build in matching coloured storage acting as a frame to the stair-well. From this room there was an intriguing staircase with a small section of old open-tread stairs leading to a white staircase that had been faced with terracotta coloured stone paint – the top storey contained a living room as well as a large glass sliding door to the balcony. It also contained a hand made wood kitchen built by his carpenter and again painted in cool green with a creamy pink marble work-surface and sink. The sink had been recovered from the building and was an inspiration for some of the colour scheme throughout the house. It was fabulous and not what would be expected from the almost colonial frontage with the wrought iron balconies.

"What condition was the house before the renovation?" – "It was a wreck, of course much work – but you see the results of this." Yes we do! -"Right onto the next house –a work in progress"

We drove through the backstreets of the town past a number of renovation projects and derelict and in some case tumble down houses fetching up outside a house which appeared to have a cloud of dust in the front yard and two workers hanging out of an upstairs window wresting with a white flexible pipe – "No –not there, that is meant to be invisible –Oh, it's a good thing I have come now!" –with that we were left in the car as he raced upstairs to give these people the benefit of his architectural training – we expected blows or at least shouting and screaming – but moments later he was back beckoning us into the house –"It's ok, it's sorted now –sometimes you are lucky enough to arrive in time – it avoids remedial work. Come in the house – it's owned by a man from Scotland –come and meet him" we all strode through the dust nodding at the guy making it with a powered jack-hammer and the other guy sitting in the cloud with him "helping"

Inside the building as our eyes adapted to coming in from the bright sunlight we met Jack who was now standing next to and staring at a collection of stone pieces laid out on the floor –a jig-saw puzzle of an eight foot gothic stone arch –there was scratching of heads and a bit of kicking at the stones at the apex to adjust the angles and a bit more staring helped by smoking. We were led upstairs by a tall man who

66

turned out to be Jack's son who was over for a few week's helping as part of a working holiday.

Once introductions had been made we were shown the stripped wooden floor and the new windows and doors upstairs –complete with bright white stone window sills –inlaid with small enamelled tiles – an Architect's detail we were told –to add interest. "He is doing a renovation for you –my Dad says he is a magician you have made a wise choice" We were starting to realise this –though I resisted admitting he was the only architect I knew for almost 2000 miles!

"Come and see the limestone floor downstairs" – we were later told the plasterer had completed this – the first one he had ever done! -it looked great.

So how long has the work been going on – "Oh some three years at least –but my Dad keeps changing what he wants –the kitchen has been moved three times and there are more rooms now" - Three years, was this another subtle Architect's lesson, this time on the importance of good planning?

We said our thanks and returned to the car.

"You saw a lot of local wood and stone in both of these houses – if you use local materials it is right and what people are used to working with. It keeps costs down if you start importing unfamiliar glass and steel products you push up costs – much can be done here" We were all for that –and about the three years –I was too hot and thirsty to bring that up at this stage –it had been a stimulating morning enough already.

"Rolling stones"

"Next I will take you to the stone masons-it is interesting" It certainly was, and if I had been an HM Factories Safety inspector it would have kept me employed for the rest of my career.

We parked −again in a cloud of dust −not all self-made, in a clear space in front of an open fronted building in the middle of what looked like the site of a recently demolished large marble building. I subsequently realised their rather random stockpiling system had given this impression and like many people's sock drawers or desks this was a carefully organised mess where some-one knew where everything was. I think he was off that day- something was said to one of the only two people visible who took a breather from hand feeding large rocks into some fearsome powered saw-bench machine that was surrounded by a mix of water spray and dust − both operatives were dressed in the standard company safety gear of designer sunglasses, shorts, sandals and heavy metal T-shirt. Though if this was your workplace −Black Sabbath or the like probably seemed quite soothing. We were shown us some different finished sheets of grey and white stone but the noise of the machinery made it virtually impossible to hear him − after waving an off-cut he had picked off the floor to stone mason/heavy metal fan number 1 and receiving a thumbs up we went outside. He seemed to have acquired a free marble cd rack and I wondered cynically if this may not have been the whole purpose of the visit −it's not every day I

68

get taken to somewhere quite so "marble less" but wisely resisted saying so. Before we left he took me over to meet a man making marked on the face of stone blocks –one at a time by hand –" it is popular he said -Crazy he said" and I must admit I wondered whether Stone Works Inc employee health care scheme covered RSI.

In car and back to the office –"they can cut anything there in stone for bathrooms, work surfaces, window sills- it all possible and not expensive. We will go back to Agios now"

We were dropped at the office we had seen so much –what next – "Tomorrow is Saturday –I will ring you Sunday to arrange meeting at the Pano house and we must have supper together-there is much to discuss" – He was not kidding!

Stunned we staggered out of their air-conditioned office into the sunlight –food and drink before anything else. We went round the corner to the café with the designer bar and bathroom that we had been in the previous May – was that only ten weeks ago –a lot had happened and I had a feeling it was only just beginning.

'Captain Kilometrico'

We went round the corner to the café in the square and sat under the sun-shades- a drink was called for there was so much to think about but our confidence in what could be achieved by our Architect was growing by the day. Food for the stomach as well as for thought –

greek salads and cheese saganaki (fried cheese) and potato omelette – a first!

Refreshed we ordered coffees and watched the world go by – we had chosen the ideal spot to do this. From experience, it seemed impossible to drive through this town without entering this square and doing at least one circuit of the roundabout planted with palm trees. There was also sufficient vegetation to make it difficult to spot the required or only accessible exit –so multiple circuits like an astronaut trapped in orbit was the norm.

As we sat enjoying the heat and watching the circuits we started monitoring the traffic- how many seat belts worn – two were spotted – not including tourist hire cars –out of scores. How many drivers were talking on phones, texting or smoking or both.

Then how many crash helmets on bikes and scooters –and if worn, how many were actually done up? The trend was bucked by a 'Captain Kilometrico' look-a-like - helmet worn, bright blue to match the moped and bucked up- he looked like the human cannon ball.

I need to describe Captain Kilometrico, he was used to promote some kind of sweets and looked like Dan Dare –with a blue helmet and lantern jaw plus an inane grin.

A few years back on a day's outing to the Lasithi plateau we stopped at a café for drinks when we spotted a human sized blue helmeted superhero plastic head sized sweet container, empty, on top of the counter and in a fit of enthusiasm bought him for several hundred drachma (around £4 at the time) Minutes later as we drove from the village we noticed the shop owner carefully collecting an identical one from the shop next door –had we spotted some international confectionary promotion counterfeit racket –who knows – now he lives in my office and grins at me from the bookshelf.

Before we paid the bill and left, the square carried another surprise. For no apparent reason the air was suddenly filled with an overpowering smell of what must be incense and moments later we spotted a dark clad priest crossing the square in a cloud of invisible incense-the traffic swerved around him!

The afternoon was spent relaxing on the beach; the time split between the sea and the shade of the trees. But that evening we returned to the little house –we needed to look at in the light of recent discussions. This time we walked from the main square up the hill and timed

70

ourselves, 20 minutes including walking backwards some of the way to appreciate the view. The house was as we left it –awaiting the return of the Albanians. There was still much to be cleared and we were anxious to get on but it was still baking hot, we didn't know the intricacies of greek dumping legislation. We sat upstairs on our sacks on top of the feta cheese tins and watched the mountains opposite become pink in the sunset. Yes, the Architect was right –it was essential to bring this view into the house- in his words- "that view is no good behind a wall"

We walked around the village –taking photos of the back wall of the house when we could catch a glimpse from one or other of the narrow alleys. It worked up a hunger for us so we followed the old donkey track down the hill, round the back of the school and back up to the next village up to our favourite restaurant. We loved their mix of mezes, fried aubergines, peppers in vinegar –grilled shrimps, feta cheese and chilly pate, stuffed vine leaves –delicious. Drinks of local wines served in the metallic jugs –copper coloured or gold or blue. All of this eaten under a canopy of vines, little lights and the stars, overlooking the lights of the town down below twinkling as reflections in the bay and the harbour.

An architect in the house

The week had seemed fairly frenetic and a little unusual spending time in offices and admiring our ruin with it's impressive complement of hay and oil drums. Perhaps there was time for a rest ?

The next days were spent sight-seeing and lazing on the beach –well it was in the mid-thirties and if your beach has an adjacent restaurant and bar it seems churlish not to respond. It had been suggested that the Architect would ring us on Sunday to arrange meeting at the house and talking further. Sunday afternoon between reading a book and floating in the sea the phone rang –"Geoff ? – , how are you – what do you both like to eat ?" – "Well, we eat most of the local dishes –like seafood and meat –though we are not big fans of offal dishes and draw the line at brains, not in my opinion, unreasonably !"

"Fine – we will meet up at the house tomorrow at 6.30 then you will come with me for supper –I know somewhere –it is my treat- see you 6.30 at the Pano house."

"OK –great, thanks –see you then."

Monday flew past – there was some more shopping and we also tracked down some kitchen showrooms and furniture shops but it seemed a little unreal looking for furniture and fittings for a house that was currently furnished with hay and industrial sized oil drum and cheese tins. Also we had to decide which room would be the bedroom or kitchen, where would the plumbing go ? Should we have a bed-sitting room, or could the kitchen be in the living room. Was a roof terrace still a possibly –we needed it for the view and where could extra windows go?

As therapy we drove back to town via Neapolis the administrative seat of the prefecture, in other words the county town and where we had first been told the price of the house and made the decision that we would embark on the course of action that had brought us to this point.

The town had a number of local shops –ironmongers, electrical goods shops and also a blacksmith who seemed to be making all sorts of shapes out of shiny and matt-black metal. There were also a huge variety of old house styles , windows, doors and balconies many of these we had photographed on previous visits but today we felt more like we were absorbing them through new eyes –trying to use them as inspiration for the Pano house – but strangely not taking any pictures – we seemed beyond that point. Back to the apartment to change –we mustn't be late to meet up at the house.

We arrived in Pano at 6.30 and parked behind the church to walk as quickly as the heat of early evening would allow. Some Pano residents were sitting outside their houses in the shade, smiles and 'Yas's' were exchanged – we must be staring to look more familiar to people – and we were now able to find our way through the muddle of alleys with only a little hesitation. He was there already sitting in the open doorway upstairs, where we were hoping that a balcony was possible with it's view down between the buildings to the bay in the distance.

We apologised for being a little late –" no problem, I came at six –I wanted to sit here and think about the house."

"So what do you think?" –I asked cautiously.

"I saw it when the survey was done – it is a good house , a great position- plenty of opportunities but because of the size it must all be done with care." Having given us this good news we then quietly looked around downstairs – "I think down here could be the bathroom and a kitchen area – but disguised, so that a hall area could be created when you first come into the house – the living area can be upstairs with a little more space from a small balcony.

"I like the stairs hatch –we would like to keep that, and the front door if possible"

The whole conversation seemed to be taking place in a reverential tone –the three of us were talking about the house as if we needed to whisper and gradually get the house itself to be ready for what we hoped would be a transformation but one that would take place without the nameless house being traumatised- it would retain it's personality. We had taken to calling 'the little house in Pano' –not in any derogatory sense but little in a charming sense. In the same way that one of our dogs had been named Boyo after "No good Boyo" in Dylan Thomas's Under Milk Wood – but he had come to assume a boyish demeanour and this has stood him in good stead in his old age when people refuse to believe he is an old dog –forever young!

Downstairs still had about a quarter of the original hay in a collection of large plastic sacks at least a dozen, each on about three foot long by two foot wide. As well as this there was the collection of whittled walking sticks at the foot of the stairs and the large earthenware jar, now at the foot of the stairs. There was also the row of pegs with some donkey tack, harnesses and a bridle –still hanging up. The donkey had maybe left in a hurry or hopefully this was some old tack no longer required?

Making our way past these treasures the three of us regrouped upstairs – "I was looking here before you came but of course, the house is completely different now you are here" –"smaller ? "– I ventured. "No, no – any house starts to assume the character of the owners – already the two of you are bringing yourselves and your plans into the house – already changing it's character."

Well changing the character would be a start –water electricity and some more windows- oh and less hay would be even better.

"Here will be the living room and we must get more light in – the large window Is good – it will provide access to a balcony without too much alteration. It is the access to the new roof that bothers me – and the new roof itself. It is not easy. There is also the view outside that we must get into the house –it cannot remain behind the wall."

74

He also briefly confused me – "You know Nietzche?" he suddenly asked.

"You mean the philosopher?" –after all the evening was taking a philosophical course.

"No, No – Niches – in the wall"

"Oh, yes "

"That is a way of getting more space into the house; these walls are nearly a metre thick in places- we can use that space –we need to be clever to gain space"

"Yes, fine –that's safe , is it?" I asked, doubtfully.

"Of course, it is normal –there is one here already –it is a good way of putting in cupboards"

We were gradually realising how spoilt for space we were at home – although our house was not an overlarge old cottage we had never considered burrowing into the walls to create space – and at times of shortage in the house we supplemented space by having places in the garden –this wasn't an option in Pano we had no garden.

I noticed the Architect was eying the ceiling – a slight exaggeration as we were all looking at the timbers below the backs of the roof tiles.

"Something may be possible by changing the roof levels –sometimes when a floor is excavated like here and the roof replaced there are things that can be done to squeeze in another floor or a mezzanine half floor –I don't know here – there is not much of a step up and there is always a risk of rain water draining from the street."

Not quite the running water we had been anticipating.

We then all started getting silly by talking of small windows to get at the view – small openings with sliding shutters –like projection windows –with the light and view coming in as he said "Boof, boof- and here, boof, boof" –rapidly splaying his outstretched fingers from his closed fist to emphasise the drama.

"The stairs –do you want stairs?"

"Well is a roof terrace still an option?"

There seemed to be a pattern here –we were answering many of his questions with a question of our own. Fortunately these ping-pong mutual interrogations were often ended by his declaration of "of course"

75

or "here it is normal" or less frequently "anything is possible"-before adding darkly – "at a price"

"I am seeing the stairs coming out of the wall, like blocks – it is possible- in this room they could be a feature – stone, or glass"

"We could put lights inside them " –"they could light up as you stood on them ..."- yes, definitely getting silly now.

Here the room would need to double as a bedroom, some sort of seating area that converts – or a bed that fold from the wall –"in a niche? –bloody big niche –would need an RSJ !"

And keeping the trap door would make the room seem bigger and cosier when closed; it needs an easy closing arrangement.

Conversation turned to the present contents that we were all averting our eyes from – three oil drums – that looked from the state of them had contained the plaster rendering that had been carried out in recent years.

An interesting but dirty pottery dish –some two foot across.

More carved sticks including long tapering curved ones in the roof –"those are used to get the olives out of the trees- keep those and we will put them back in –you need to respect contents" –(I hoped this wouldn't extend to the oil drums!)

A large wooden crate stood at the head of the stairs. It was debated whether it dated from the days of the Imperial flying boats that pre-war flew from Britain to Cairo and beyond serving the British empire. One was still in Mirabello bay where they had crash-landed – they must have been quite a sight from Pano where they would be visible like great sea birds landing in the lagoon. The crashed one was still in the bay and the crew buried in the local graveyard.

At the corner of the road up to the apartments was the Imperia restaurant –now closed but peering through the window you could see framed prints of the Imperial flying boats. It was reputed that Winston Churchill had once over-nighted here as had Mahatma Ghandi –presumably not the same night!

He had seen crates from that time 70 years ago still used as storage in local houses – a brief examination seemed to reveal no identifying marks- a task for later investigation. There was a quandary about how demanding to be about the house clearance with such potential 'treasures' to be considered. As I have said before: there was much to think about – we left the house leaving the door which in passing we agreed should be salvaged- to walk back through the alleyways, casting a backward glance down the street towards the bay and across to the distant mountains that were starting to turn their characteristic evening candy pink colour –breath-taking. Yes-we must bring that view into the house somehow.

We loaded the ceramic bowl and a small collection of walking sticks into the company jeep – they were going to his storeroom for safety. We would have liked to take the large urn but even if we could have carried it we were assured us it was safe in the house and would be viewed as a fixture or fitting –"all houses have one –it belongs with the house" I would have preferred a water tank and drains –still.

Crosby and Mash

The plan had been that we would go together for dinner but the venue had yet to be agreed. Meeting up was proposed on the coast road in the car park of a large hotel that we vaguely knew –he said he needed a half an hour to record some thoughts. We went back to change and shower –the little house was pretty dusty and dirty –not sure how much domestic help the donkey had in there.

We drew into the car park and spotted the Jeep and it's grinning occupant who also seemed to have changed but he waved us to follow him – and half a mile later we turned into an even larger hotel car park – are we eating here ?

Well he said it was his treat – but no –he led us into a grand reception, ultra modern with much polished marble and limestone, a twelve foot aquarium set into the reception desk and a myriad of low voltage lights set in the floor and the ceiling.

"I thought you would like to see this – the décor is interesting but more interesting is the permanent art exhibition in the grounds – there are almost a hundred sculptures and installations commissioned by world class artists. As dusk fell we wandered around the grounds-leading down to the sea, admiring the works. Some were spectacular some were frankly honkers but all were interesting. "This is open to the public-there is a catalogue, come back and view at your leisure. The hotel abuts a public beach bring a picnic and have a swim –no-one will mind, I swam here as a boy before the hotel was built"

Very Crete !
"Follow me, the restaurant is near the hospital-it is traditional food – well-cooked."

At the restaurant we were welcomed by an impressively moustached maitre de who reminded me of David Crosby once he smiled. The Architect took the menu and said he would order for us – and a selection of mezes were ordered, vegetable and meat and fish. There was some intense discussion in greek with the CSN tribute band waiter and laughter –I hoped there wasn't a plot to disguise a traditional compulsory brains dish for new householders.
We drank the local wine and talked about the house and the options – the imaginations started to run riot again – "I think the kitchen could be a mobile unit that has the services connected by flexible hoses and is wheeled out and put away when not required."
"Would this be in a niche?"
There was more talk of the view – I have done a house with an infinity pool"
"So in view of space constraints- could we have an infinity sink –it would avoid the need to descend two flights of stairs – including one that would execute an impromptu light show!"
The food interrupted the reverie and I needn't have worried –when it arrived it was wonderful and no sign of brains. Though there was a strange dish which we think we identified as some kind of pickled bulb which we concluded was hyacinth. It had a strange sort of chemical taste –I resisted seconds.

Over the meal the Architect suddenly "I am bothered about the roof"
Do you definitely think you need a flat roof terrace. I admitted that this was one aspect that had bothered me –from the front the proportions of the house looked so right and I wasn't sure what effect the flat roof would have on these proportions or how this could be managed. The main priority is to have a space to enjoy the view – if we can manage a small dining area for say six that would be fine. Sighs of relief all round.

Insurance

Before we left again for home we had a few things to do. The most pressing was a visit to the Insurance company office. This had been discussed earlier in the year when we had raised the subject with the agent. I suppose it might appear somewhat overcautious: the house was virtually empty, (though the hay could be a fire hazard); the windows had no glass in and the door had no obvious means of locking. We had originally been amused by what looked like a Hornby clock-work train key apparently rusted in the door. Quaint, we had thought but now the recent burden of ownership in the Mediterranean, almost 2000 miles from home, was starting to weigh more heavily on us. Other questions had arisen – like our liability if the house did catch fire – and spread up the terrace and through the narrow streets- what sort of uninsured liability would we have? We could never return but Greece is in the EU we could be pursued through the courts – or extradited and put in prison with English plane spotters! It was decided, we must have insurance and could we possibly arrange it before we left –tomorrow!!

Of course, this would be easy said the reassuring voice of the agent at the office. We could see George at his Insurance office across the square –we were given the name of the hotel next-door – was this a more upmarket area? No adjacent cheese shops – would this increase or reduce the premium – should we shop around – no time, no local knowledge? An appointment was made for us at 7 p.m. the same evening, bring your passports, some euros, and the papers relating to the house. Given that we had yet to establish an address for the house any policy would ,we felt, require careful wording.

Nevertheless, early evening found us back in the town square looking for the insurance offices. Although it was early evening the sun was still very hot and we walked in the shade until we found what we assumed was the office. We entered and introduced ourselves to a tall young man lounging in a chair staring at the screen of his silent mobile phone. We explained that George was expecting us at seven – we were shown into a second office where George presided over a large desk laden with papers. The office seemed opulent and cluttered with a strong smell of polished wood, most of which appeared to be generously covered with papers. George stood up and shook hands, we were offered two chairs in front of the desk and asked how he could help us. We explained we were recent owners of a small, un-modernised house in Pano and felt we needed insurance before returning to England, for peace of mind …..he grinned and stood up, what would you like to drink – cold orange ? Yes please.

"Adonis", he slunk in from the outer office. "Two iced oranges, now" Adonis disappeared but returned shortly with two large glasses of freshly squeezed orange juice with ice. I began to wonder just how expensive insurance was in Crete. In over thirty years of holding UK bank accounts I had never been offered so much as a suckie sweet!

"Now your 'spitty', your house, I mean. What do you want insuring? This was quite a question, it wasn't so much a matter of insuring the house – there weren't really any contents, only the large Greek urn and the stairs –oh, and the pointy stick collection, oh yes, and the rest of the hay –though if that could be stolen –no questions asked - it would be more than ok.

Our main concern, I explained, in the short term was any damage that our house might do to a third party, by perhaps falling on them or catching fire – I realised this seemed alarmist as it had stood for decades possibly several centuries, we just didn't know. But that was before anyone started messing with it putting in glass staircases and dynamiting rocks to put in drains. Yes he understood – let's look at the deeds. We handed them over and also showed him some photos of the house. "Is there a standard sort of policy that we could review once we have possessions and the house is renovated - I mean it's a bit strange as there is no security at present like locks, or glass- but on the other hand the hazards of water or electricity have yet to be introduced to the building."

Georgios shuffled his papers and fired up his flat screen pc monitor that had been hidden behind a pile of books. With one eye on our deeds the other on a keyboard, pausing only to suck his frappe or iced coffee unless it was a Tia Maria based cocktail to enliven the world of insurance -he entered some particulars.

"We can do all of this and then revisit it when you have finished your renovations –of course, the house will be more valuable then." Was I been softened up for some huge bill – A house with no security, needing extensive renovation, absentee landlords – I couldn't help imagining what the Norwich would be quoting. Pehaps he was drinking cocktails; maybe George drank them all day and Adonis. That would explain his lethargy.

After asking us a few more questions George dramatically hit a final key on the pc and pushed the keyboard to one side. " Adonis!!" – movement was heard outside and Adonis ambled in with a printed document. George flourished it – "your policy" a copy each.

It was impressively printed on one side of A4 with a coloured heading. There did not seem to be a lot of small print but what there was was all in Greek, I should not have been surprised.

I have the document in front of me – written on the back in pencil is the capturing of a few key points as George ran through it rapidly:-

o Fire, including smoke
o Damage from outside
o Damage by fire to electrical fittings
o Flood
o Storage after fire
o Cleaning after fire (to € 1000)
o Windows broken
o Shooting from road (? !!)
o Subsidence (€ 500 excess)
o Fire from next door
o Theft when in residence

And the bill € 8274 !!!!
WHAT !!!!!...........Oh hang on, €82.74 –or about £56 –that seems very fair – does that include the drinks.
We paid , shook hands promised to update him on renovations and

left, without waking up Adonis.

We could now return to England safe in the knowledge that we had taken steps to protect our investment –I think?

Sunday Times August 7th – Crete –is this the new Costa Brava? God I hope not !

The article described the increasing popularity of Crete for residence and holiday homes amongst the British. Ruined houses are fetching 40 or £50,000 –don't we know it – so are we just part of a trend ?

Hi to everyone...

We are safely back in Sussex -and it's sunny.

Thanks for everyone's time and care during our recent visit - we are even more excited about the little house project after talking with you(if that is possible!!)

We have been looking at the Grand Designs exhibition brochures and some of our old design books - so will be contactin g soon with some ideas.

We did speak to Maria the previous owner before leaving - she mentioned clearing the house Saturday - and said she had been speaking to you in the office but we think she will need some pushing.

We also left a card for the neighbours but met a german lady who moved to Pano a year ago and lives in Paris and knows your work and was very complementary about you all.

She thought our neighbour is a Greek who is married to a french lady but lives in Paris and will be back in september - so that may be helpful.

On one of my photos it seems that upstairs there is nothing against the back wall - it is over a single storey building -so - perhaps an exterior glass stair well or if not glass block stairs set into wall with light coming through ?

Will be in touch again soon

Geoff

Thanks very much -the topographic survey arrived today together with your pretty card - thank you. We are having lots of ideas and will be sending you some material soon We are finding some interesting stuff and will go to some good bookshops we know next week We hope you have a good weekend also

Best regards

Geoff

Thank you for your nice e-mail.

We have now sent to you the topographic survey.

I have taken note of the information you have passed me regarding your

neighbours and will make a search too.

Maria, the vendor, told us the house would be cleaned this weekend.

Every bit of information you send me is welcome.

I wish you both a very good weekend.

E

Architect

Hi everyone

Hope you are all well and happy

Still sunny in England (shock!)

We are putting together a lot of cuttings from books, magazines and photos and should be sending them to you shortly -I will try scanning and emailing -will see how big it is -could zip it I guess.

We have also bought two japanese style books:-

SMALL SPACES -Azby Brown ISBN 4-7700-2084-8
And
THE VERY SMALL HOME - Azby Brown and KENGO KUMA ISBN4-7700-2999-3

Do you know them - though I guess you have seen much more Japanese style first hand.If you don't have them I could post them.

Well -I will get back to constructing the document -all the best -I hope the weekly market is full of people this morning selling large black plastic bags of hay (and old oil drum and almonds!)

Hay, Hay

Thank you for your nice e-mail.
We have now sent to you the topographic survey.
I have taken note of the information you have passed me regarding your neighbours and will make a search too.
Maria, the vendor, told us the house would be cleaned this weekend.
Every bit of information you send me is welcome.
I wish you both a very good weekend.
E

Dear E.
After gathering together the ideas pictures so far we have put a copy in the post as scanning/emailing using our domestic copier/scanner is likely to be a long task. Should reach you early next week
All the best
Geoff

Good afternoon from Crete
I hope that both of you are fine there.
Very hot here at the moment.
I was on the phone now with Maria in Pano and she had some problems these
days with her job and it was not possible to take off the things from the house. She apologises for the delay and promised me that she will do so this weekend.

F

Thanks F
Nice to speak again - we were just anxious that the neighbours may
return and see all this mess of bags of hay if it had not been cleared.
We are looking forward to coming back for two weeks on 6th september which is not long now. For the second week we have some
very good friends of ours coming to Crete for the first time so we will
bring them in and see if they want to buy a house

Good morning - hope you are all well on the island.
We are hopeful that you will have heard that the house has been
cleared -and particularly the street outside because we do not think it
will help with any negotiations about windows etc if the french/greek
neighbours return and find all the bags in the street.
We know you are doing your best -many thanks
Let us know when clear

We look forward to seeing you after the 6th September

Ps I have forwarded the details of the house for renovation in Pano to
some friends of ours who were looking at property in Crete as well as
the link to your site

Hi - hope you are all well -will see you next week arriving on 6th Sept
really looking forward to it -any news on the clearance of the bags of
hay?
Thanks
Geoff

Thanks for your e-mail and we are all well.
The hay has been removed from inside and outside the house, so
please do not worry
any more about that. The barrels are still there and these will be removed once we start
the renovation.
Best wishes.

F

Thanks for that - it's a relief -it was the blocking of the path that worried us -as we will want to negotiate with them and the sacks would
not have helped, the drums are no problem -we won't be moving in
just yet -
See you next week !!
Thanks again
Geoff

The removal of the hay was certainly a huge relief as the thought of
our new neighbours arriving for a stay to be confronted by umpteen
cubic metres of hay all bagged up in black plastic forming a barrier six
or seven foot high between them and their garden –let's just say it
won't be helpful in possible future negotiations over windows etc.

Clearing the house

We returned again in September, hoping that temperatures would have cooled a bit from the heat of July. It still seemed very warm but there was a breeze and we felt optimistic that this trip would at least see some progress in the plans and we might also see how much bigger the house was without the hay inside it.

Early evening found us walking again through the alleys of the village, down the steps and round the corner to the little house- and, yes, the bags of hay had gone, as had been promised- excellent.

We could now remind ourselves what else had been acquired with the house in the way of contents. Before describing the clearing of the house I will remind you of the inventory of the contents earlier in the year. I emphasise, that it was not the fixtures and fittings list that 'swung the deal.'

Firstly, several cubic yards of hay - thankfully, now all gone!
Secondly, the pithori –the huge earthenware vase –that was going nowhere –it had taken two of us to move it downstairs and into the corner of the room. Assorted treasures, specifically a large earthenware bowl and a collection of hand carved walking sticks both now kindly removed by Manos to the storeroom at the office.

Additionally, from memory there seemed to be at least four full sized oil drums, several large feta cheese tins, one large wooden crate, a second smaller wooden box, and alarmingly none of these known to be empty! There was also a further collection of hand-whittled sticks – length mixed plus assorted sacks. Some of the sacks were full of other stuff – in some cases more sacks!

This seemed a rather large collection for a house of only two small rooms. There was certainly some clearing to do – better get started.
In view of the temperature the plan was to attack the house early evening in the couple of hours before darkness. There was a secondary benefit to this timing that would only become apparent once we started. Once inside we opened up the shutters and took stock, (and a deep breathe.) We needed some space – and the only way to do that was to start chucking stuff out. There was a 'washing line' stretched across the room upstairs with some sacks pegged to it –this was taken

down –and rolled up into the plastic sacks we had brought to remove stuff. Anything else that looked to be rubbish upstairs was also put in sacks and the first trip of many was made to the large green municipal bin a stroll of a couple of hundred yards away in the small car park behind the church. In the rabbit warren of narrow streets there was a choice of routes once we had left our own dead end alley-way. This was to prove useful as well as varying the scenery on what was to be the first of many trips to the bin.

To make real space upstairs we needed to move the oil drums and to do this they needed emptying. The first one was half full of almond nuts –in their shells and of indeterminate age. Trying one by breaking between two handy stones it seemed very dry and old – I am not really keen on fresh almonds – so they were bagged up to go.

Working in the evening meant we got to meet more of the villagers and unintentionally, provide them with entertainment. There seemed a certain amount of intrigue as to what we were throwing out or maybe what the previous owner had kept in the house ? Working out that the largest group of observers were sitting at the top of our alleyway and (advantageously nearer the house than the bin) anything they showed sufficient interest in to take would be one less load to the bin and could dramatically slash the clearance time. The first victory was the green plastic netting –one roll of new, one used. This was seized on by one of the ladies of uncertain age who I discovered lived on the corner near the church and who I later exchanged enthusiastic observations, mostly in sign language, on the quality of the sunset. We believe the netting was put under the olive and carob trees to gather the crop once the trees had received something of a beating with sticks. We also had some of these sticks but they were safely tucked away in the rafters and not part of phase one of the house clearance.

The 'free issue' of the nets now added a greater air of expectancy to my trips to the bin, at least as far as the audience was concerned. This combined with their amusement at my increasingly red face and sweaty appearance given that the evening temperature was still hovering in the high twenties! Though they had mostly adopted the uniform of ladies of a certain age everywhere of cardigans – this seasons colour being black !

I learned that it was necessary in the heat to vary contents between absolute rubbish, which meant the long walk; some rubbish allowing a half-load for the majority of the walk to the bin and desirable stuff such as the for-mentioned netting, feta cheese tins, and bags of almonds - allowing a quick return and more than halving the journey time although sometimes there was the need to emphasise that these items were 'freebies' and no payment was expected –unless, and the thought has only just occurred to me, they were expecting me to pay them for recycling this junk –hmmm! The cheese tins along with the large olive oil tins were often recycled on the island as planters usually after a coat of paint to match the front door or windows. This particular victory was short lived as on the next trip the feta tins were given back to me –maybe no paint or the wrong brand of tin with limited street-cred , who knows ? I was flagging so after a quick drink of a canned beer we had brought with us and declining an invite into Maria's kafenion due to reasons of sweat and filth (ours) we called it a day –planning to return the next day. The ladies of the village settling down in their chairs in the street bid us "kalispera."

The next day we started the clearing earlier –in the heat of the afternoon! We parked the car at the back of the church as usual and walked to the house – opening up the door and shutters. It felt cooler than outside although I knew from bitter experience a few minute sweeping or carrying would change that. It also looked more spacious, not surprisingly considering the pile of junk that had been removed. It was just possible to start to envisage it becoming a habitable home –just!

After the first few walks to the large green bin that served the whole village and lived behind the church (and impressively was emptied daily!) I concluded that some mechanisation of the whole process was needed.

I had seen the occasional vehicle go through the narrow alleyways – certainly the travelling shop – a large pick-up, admittedly a battered one had been seen passing through, so it had to be possible. Also I was conscious that we still had four oil drums in the house and this seemed at least three or possibly four too many. My plan was to carefully drive the hire car as near as I could to the end of the street and load up the old oil drums and anything else I could and drive it all back through the narrow alleys. The plan went well for the first two oil drums although some very careful seventeen point turns were required. To speed this up further I decided to cautiously reverse the car to collect –then drive back out of the village –avoiding the need to turn in the desperately narrow streets.

My initial smugness at this new route was dealt a savage blow by an awful scraping as I negotiated the last corner backwards- I gingerly pulled forward and got out – the damage, despite the expensive noise seemed to be limited to a broken glass in the drivers door mirror-phew. Though after the last oil drum I reverted to trips to the bin on foot!

The next day when I called in the car hire office to report the damage it seemed that bad news travels fast –"It's OK I was told –it's only the glass"- how did they know? Small world I guess.

The house was now more or less clear. Certainly compared to the wealth of 'contents' we had inherited. The hay was gone, most of the oil drums–the last one with a hinged lid remained as storage (and because I couldn't risk the hire car through the streets again-not with only one mirror)

The large clay urn stood in the corner downstairs, upstairs was one hinged wooden box that served as a make-shift bench and was named the snail box (because some snail shells had been found inside) Also the large wooden crate remained to provide a rough table –it also was to big to leave by the stairs or window and still provided some mysterious question as to how it had ever got there!

Now there was a chance to clean up a bit.

The floor needed another good brush out, upstairs and downstairs and there was a chance to give the floorboards upstairs a good scrub, they were beautiful and at least a foot wide. We were so pleased with it we wanted to show it off to friends and whilst the lack of facilities i.e. water, electricity and drainage definitely precluded any dinner parties we were at least ready to show the house to someone, hell, we could even provide eats and drinks if we brought them with us and didn't plan to wash up, or sit down on chairs!

George's House

Conversations with George who ran two businesses in the town revealed two interesting facts. Firstly, that not only had his grandfather owned a house in the village where George as a child, together with his family, often had Sunday lunches, en famille. More amazingly, George was potentially a neighbour of ours and owned a property in the village- this was news. It was arranged that on the next afternoon we would meet up in the square and go up to the village to view both properties. We started to play down ours to George, describing the work required and all the features it lacked. All he would say in reply was "wait till you see mine!"

On the next day we met George and his girlfriend in the square –it was hot, of course, they were on a motorbike; George generously having donated the crash helmet to his girlfriend. We would follow them up the hill in our little hire car. His credentials as a local were confirmed en route when they veered off the road onto the cobbled donkey track. We had no choice but to follow them as we knew the village, although not large, was a jumble of narrow streets and alleyways. We stood a good chance of not finding them or their house. I can only imagine the ride on the bike as we were pleased after several hundred yards to rumble and rattle to a halt in a small parking area under some large spreading trees. We followed George until he stood in front of a ruined wall in a small garden that looked to be almost entirely rockery. " This is my house" he said , casually waving towards the wall and a small stone, single storey building attached to it. "There were two rooms but ......" his sentence ended unfinished and hung in the silence. We all entered the other room – it was dark and would have been darker had there not been a large hole in the roof through which a tree had grown. "It needs some work "said George. He then reminisced about family lunches in the garden, the area now littered with large stones from the collapsed walls. The house has been divided he said and pointed to the adjoining building which seemed to have a complete roof. "that belongs to my cousin, we are in dispute about repairs as well as the boundaries- it is difficult with families"

I searched for some words of reassurance, "It will be a good little house – with views to the sea....and you have plenty of stones to use for repairs...." It sounded like faint praise and helpfully George rescues me. "Come on let's go and see you house –I do not know it."

93

We walked up through the village with several stops to exchange greetings with people known to George.

As we neared our house an elderly lady accosted George and spoke rapidly to him whilst gesticulating towards a narrow alleyway.

George explained that she wanted George to show us a house at the end of the alleyway that her family was selling. "Come on we'll have a look- it might be interesting." A large ancient wooden door was pushed open and with our small torch we could see two large rooms with a large curved archway between them. As it did not benefit from George's style of roof ventilation and we couldn't see any windows we made polite noises and returned down the alleyway. As we walked round the corner towards our house I enquired of George what had been said to him. It was along the lines of "would your foreign friends like to buy a house?" He had asked the price and was told to make an offer so he thought he might come back with a better torch and avoid the family property dispute he was in. I took the opportunity to ask George what the general opinion was of Cretans towards foreigners buying holiday homes on the island. His view was that Cretans were generally pragmatic about it, he said a lot of the houses were not con-sidered suitable for modern living. Thinking of our lack of services it was difficult to contest this view. He further said that if the houses were not bought and left empty then they could just fall down – having so recently seen his inheritance it was difficult to argue with this statement. Still it seemed to bear out our experience of a positive re-action to our telling local friends that we had bought a house for restoration. I guess most families had some businesses that would see the benefit from such sales and subsequent works.

We reached our house and opened the door and the upstairs shutter to let the light in. Although we were aware of the major works that were needed we felt quite proud of the little house – it looked larger no some of the old "contents" had been removed. Also the lack of trees growing through the roof and opening windows definitely gave it the edge over the other two village properties we had been inside that day! George and Marianna made complimentary comments and over-looking the lack of basic services or glass in the windows George de-clared that if it were his he would move in straight away and borrow water and power from a neighbour! This seemed to round off an inter-esting afternoon and we were left with this thought as we said our goodbyes to each other.

Plans

It was arranged that we would meet up at the house with the architect. This was to be the second meeting at the house with Manos. We wanted to talk through making the roof terrace area private whilst at the same time bringing in light.

The heights were roughly measured out and a rough estimation was made on the back wall as to how many and how high any stairs would be up to the proposed roof terrace. Our general preference was to retain as much as possible of the original features in the house but to also put in modern features and to bring in more light.

As we talked about this it was becoming clear to us that some of the features such as the original stairs may be a step too far. This may bring other opportunities to re-use the old wood for other features or fittings. There were some old wooden shutters with the characteristic Mediterranean weathering on a blue/green paint so that the grain was coming through – that had some definite possibilities.

Even in this climate with the sun and holiday mood optimism a finished home –particularly one with fully functioning plumbing, seemed a very long way off. I think we needed to view George's home again to cheer us up – at least we had four walls!

It was hard for us to picture the house, at this stage anyway, as a completed project. The front of the house was a pale coloured rough stone facing a house opposite across an alleyway that was only two metres wide.

On the ground floor the only opening was the front door which was very weathered uncoloured wood. At floor level to the right of the door was a small opening, less than a foot square that later turned out to be a rudimentary cat flap, confirmed when a cat shot out of it during a later visit. Still, it could be the solution for any problems with vermin and avoid the use of Costos's weaponry - think positively.

As you entered the house the ground floor room was fairly gloomy with the only light coming through the doorway.

The room itself was roughly four meters by four meters with no real features apart from the debris left in there. On the right hand side, behind the open door was a stone step up which continued right across the right hand wall and was the start point for the wooden staircase. This was a rough wooden 'ladder-like' stairs that seemed solid enough and provided the way upstairs through a hatch cut out of the upstairs floor boards which handily doubled up as a ceiling to the ground floor. The floor boards were laid across some ceiling beams of different depths and set at irregular distances from each other. Once we opened the shutters upstairs the limited light that leaked down the stairs gave us the chance to get a better look at downstairs. The step across the wall seemed peculiar –perhaps it was structural; the house was on a slight slope, down to the left. The ceiling was higher than we first thought. We were used to low ceilings as we lived in an old cottage at home in Sussex and this was higher than that – good! With the door open we were able to measure the thickness of the walls –more than two foot wide-this would lead to much discussion on the subject of 'niches' but more of that later.

 After the discussions at the house we reconvened for supper and further discussions about the house. Manos met us in the square to go up to the restaurant – his opening words were surprising –"I have been thinking about the bathroom – it could sit in the corner of the room – like a white egg! The stairs would be cut into the top and provide the access to upstairs." I wonder if he expected not unnatural opposition – but we were intrigued –"Yes, combining the stairs and bathroom –brilliant! Would it be difficult to construct?"'"Yes, of course!" said Manos – "it may not be possible –and would require much supervision......" I detected he may be back-pedalling on this –surprised by our all too ready acceptance.

"Let's go and eat- we are a long way from constructing the bathroom."
This was true.

There was a difficult moment in the restaurant when Manos produced
a bottle of wine from his bag and asked if it was ok for it to be opened
–the typical response –"Of course, as long as I can have some" not, I
suggest the average response in any restaurant in Sussex.

Drawings were made on scraps of paper as the meal progressed and
the wine flowed.

Some of the planning was very random –like a stream of conscious-
ness – we had talked to each other about our broad requirements –
they were more of a feeling for the place – not specifics. They included
–light – white and colours – the use of any recovered materials from
the little house- a mix of old and new but a stripped or pared down
look to make the small size workable -multi-functional furniture –
bringing in the view – a private roof area- with views- a discrete bathroom – air-con unit to provide additional cooling.

Manos also had some early thoughts :-

a roof terrace for part of the roof –perhaps cut-in
- stone stairs from the wall
- gaining height as the building was currently below the 7 metre
maximum that was permitted in the village a possible height
gain of a metre and a half
- to have a roof that is not 'all a roof' –giving indirect light
- without re-inforcement it would be possible to gain space with
niches supplying cupboards for storage
- use the double door upstairs as a balcony
- no solar panel on the roof – a pumped water system installed
with the tank
- create a double bed from two seats
- colour the steps and incorporate them as furniture
- some means to gain the view
- paint ceiling beams but keep the grain
- bathroom and kitchen downstairs
- holes for light ?
- match new ground floor window to door and first floor window.

We all started 'brainstorming' ideas – could the kitchen be a mobile
unit on wheels – the dining table could fold down from the wall with a
painting on the back – his carpenter could make furniture to our speci-

97

fication – local blacksmiths were very creative. When thinking of a kitchen we could consider using niches for wall cupboards – and even for fridges, maybe two small ones instead of one large one
the floor downstairs needed to provide light – light tiles or terrazzo.

Once we settle on some plans and building consents are obtained then a contract would be drawn up to specify what would be done.
It all seemed possible or at least started to feel a possibility. These discussions always seem less beset with problems if they are had under the stars, in a warm climate after a good meal in good company accompanied by a glass or two of wine. Yeah – no worries.
Of course in the cold light of day and the next time we were up at the house looking at the four bare, dusty walls – with the gloom relieved by shafts of light through the glassless windows and pinpricks of light between the roof tiles – it definitely looked more daunting! Also why were there so many other derelict houses in the village? Why weren't the narrow alleyways full of skips and scaffolding ?
We regained our optimism –we must be ahead of the curve –again!
Once every property was renovated and the whole village developed we wouldn't have been able to afford a house here so we were being sensible –prudent even –for a change !
Fired up with enthusiasm for the house we started to explore the right sort of shops and suppliers. I have to tell you the greeks are well up on the bathroom and plumbing supplies. Tiles and flooring is also very advanced !! If there was room for a luxury Italian designer kitchen (which there isn't) we would be spoilt for choice. Some of the furniture shops were also pretty fabulous –let's hope they deliver –there's a limit to the load capacity of a hired Fiat Punto.

Nikos –and his Mum!

On a later visit to the house –and no doubt on one of my many trips to the municipal wheelie bin we met another neighbour who introduced himself as Nikos – he lived next door but one.

The next day we saw him in the town with a small boy – Nikos appeared to be in his seventies or at least late sixties – it must be his grandson.

We next met in the road around the corner from the house where he gestured to us to sit at the table next to him at the kafenion. We mentioned that we had seen him in town –indicating a small boy –he beamed and from what we could gather indicated it was his great grand son –it was a good introduction –we were then introduced to his wife and what we understood to be his Mum – who we think owned the kafenion and must be in her nineties –making Maria appear a mere newcomer to Cretan bar owning ! The afternoon was toasted in a re-strained fashion with orangina – perhaps some secret elixir of life, who knows –they all looked well on it.

Good news, Manos has had a discussion with the planning authorities and explained he had some 'questions about a small renovation project!'

The conclusion was excellent –in his words. The planners were very supportive about the proposals and even would agree to a flat roof sun terrace-apparently a significant concession in the village. There would be no problem with the minor parts of the proposals – a new ground floor window next to the front door was accepted. The balcony on the first floor was similarly agreed but the proposal he was most excited about was the agreement to raise the building roof-line by some one and a half metres. This would allow the proposed roof terrace to be contained within the building and make stair access a much more ele-gant proposition. He said that they were intrigued that people consid-ered such a small house to be of sufficient interest to renovate and he gained the impression that the renovation would be watched by them with interest!

Greek School

We began to realise that we would enjoy the village life and appreciate the island more if we could understand and speak at least some Greek. We did not underestimate the challenge as the alphabet is, to say the least, mildly confusing for someone with half a century's familiarity with the twenty-six letters of the English alphabet. We would make an effort and followed up our brief experiments with some language tapes with serious enquiries about Greek classes.

This put in train a series of events that the week before Christmas found us with minor speaking parts (in Greek) in the first nativity play I found myself in since the late 1950's, a gap of almost half a century!

Yes, we were both enrolled in a Friday night two hour class in a Greek church almost an hour away from home on the south coast. Mr Bouras the church caretaker welcomed us and led us into the classroom which was at the back of the church. It was full of old-fashioned school desks lined up in pairs – and all about eighteen inches from the ground.

As the other pupils arrived it started to feel like being back in Crete – there was an air of activity, people chattering rapidly all exaggerated by much of it happening a foot below my eye level – it appeared that the other pupils ranged from approximately 4 to 12! The adults were parents delivering them. It transpired that two of the mums were staying as well and our names were on stickers on the desk – in Greek which was why I didn't recognise it!

A number of the children were very Greek looking, some less so – two children had been brought by their mum to make them watch less television –and they were also learning mandarin!

I was sure I would have enough trouble learning Greek.

The room was like an old-fashioned school-room with a blackboard and bookcases of biblical and ordinary children's stories in Greek and I had to sit 'side-saddle' as my knees wouldn't go under the desk.

The teacher was a tall lady called Eleni who was a Greek Cypriot studying and teaching in Sussex and the teaching text was apparently used in schools in Greece. We were several terms behind the rest of the class and I was still unfamiliar with the alphabet.

After an hour at six o clock, we broke for snack-break. I was exhausted for which I felt rather guilty as most of the class had already spent five full days in a class-room that week and in some cases were not far off their bed-time!

The snacks varied week to week. Sometimes, there was a Greek theme – halva or spicy cakes – other times it was ham sandwiches, (The word for sandwich is very similar in greek!) I guess it is a modern invention in their span of history. The break times were also a chance to chat with other pupils comparing the complexities of modern greek and mandarin, or mobile phone spec with an eight year old or what was best about a greek island holiday compared with other destinations.

Much later ...

On dull winter's Saturday afternoon the phone at home in Sussex rang..."Hello, it's Manos – what is your fax number – I have some draft plans for you to consider."

"Fabulous, can you email them as a soft copy – or scan and mail" as usual technology sprang to attempt to thwart us – "Ah there is a problem - we have changed our scanner and at the moment it is a paper copy and I have not used the new scanner –I am alone in the office." We could imagine Manos's large brown eyes behind his glasses atop a crestfallen face. We desperately wanted to see the plans as soon as we could . "Hang on , I used to have an efax number that I could use to route faxes to my pc. Give me half an hour to sort it out – I'll call you back."

A frantic half hour followed which allowed me to sort out the efax and shortly after that I rang Manos at the   office and of course, got the answer phone – was he still there ? would we get the plans this weekend or have to wait until Monday ?

I checked my email inbox every few minutes over the next hour until – IT ARRIVED – all seven pages of them – two the same !! He must have been as excited as us – or he also had a new fax machine!

At the Architect's Office

We returned to the island in May of the next year, anxious to progress with the planning permission for the renovations. It was 30 degrees on the thermometer in the marina car park and felt hotter. On our first visit to the new office we had a new technique explained to us for learning greek by Manos turned 'language teacher.' It apparently consisted of taking an English word that was likely to have one or more greek roots; then, in his words, as fellow intellectuals, we would dissect the word and "follow it" as it led to other greek words. This would be both instructive and entertaining. I suffered a slight crisis of confidence after I asked him if he had often used this technique. He said that he had recently tried it with another client who refused to take it seriously. I assured him that we would be taking it seriously but we had digressed or been diverted? We had come to the office to catch up with news on the elusive planning officer.

"I have been hunting him" – not very successfully, it transpired- "he has left the island for the day."

The subject was rapidly changed and we were asked if we like hare. Some confusion followed as the male members of architectural practice were in the habit of frequently changing the design of the facial hair- designer stubble, beards, half beards, pointy star-trek sideboard designs-very Prince or George Michael (well he has greek origins). We quickly realised this was a culinary question." I have three – fresh from my brother. I will cook them for us before you go. His brother must be the hunter in the family –I wonder how he is with planning officers? Earlier visits to the office had resulted in gifts of fine wine, a great green tomato chutney and greek music cd's and music recommendations –so we weren't really surprised by the hare.

This morning the office was busy –two other customers were in and the large printer was pushing out some A2 sized plans – "these are to discuss with the planner again"-it seemed a little last minute but I wisely decided against saying so. I recalled in the dim past hovering over a printer before rushing into yet another boardroom and attempting a calm and "well-prepared" presentation". I countered our anxiety by giving him a word of greek origin to disassemble.

We had needed stamps –"what about philately?"

His interest aroused – paper and pencil were produced....."please follow me " – but he remained seated. We knew from experience that this was the introduction to an explanation –not an invite to leave the office –(apart from the occasion when we had to follow him to the church next door) –the exception that proved the rule?

I hoped that this explanation wasn't keeping the planner waiting.

I will spare you the details.

Suddenly in mid flow the planning meeting was remembered- "I must go – we can talk later over supper. And I have the hare to organise" – I mental picture of the hares I had seen in the past flashing through cornfields , standing, boxing – this seemed a good metaphor for the planning process – "yes, I will have to be delicate with the planner- it is not easy – like organising a hare."

"I will go –stay here –or go –as you like- I will see you later" In a flurry of rolled up plans and a swish of his shouldered brief-case he was gone.

The office was immediately more tranquil. We looked out the window at the harbour, browsed some books and architectural magazines and drank fresh frappes.

The time passed quickly and he returned –

"Progress, I think. He says the plans are interesting but asks me –'what are you really doing?'

"I tell him the plans are what we are doing- They are the plans!"

"He says –'for example you say that the floor is sound – but the house is old - is it really sound?'

We have agreed that he will come to the house –that is good –then he can understand about bringing the view into the house – it will allow him to make better sense of it all" That would be at least one of us then.

"Friday at 8 o'clock –can you be there?"

"8 o'clock –in the morning?" I ask.

"Yes, of course –in the morning"

"Fine, yes we will be there."

Progress indeed – perhaps.

"So, Friday the house –then at the weekend I am at an architect's conference in the city."

I said that we had planned to go to the city to look at furniture and fittings in the larger suppliers.

"Good, we can meet- I will escape from the conference."

" So we have a day off from each other tomorrow, we can use it to think of some new words to disassemble"

-"No, tomorrow I am bringing in the camera to lend you- I am not using it and you can record the house , it has a wide-angle lens. So see you tomorrow"

There was to be no rest from each other !

Meeting the Planner

We awoke early, excited and anxious –we would go to the house before eight; open the shutters and let some air in, perhaps it would be
cooler then. Driving through the town at 7.30 it was starting to come
alive. The roads and pavements were wet from the daily visit of the
cleaning lorry – people were washing cars and pavements. I contemplated collecting footage for Southern water to show them proper water use in a dry climate!

No matter we had pressing business. The far end of the town was even
busier – it was market day. Many of the older residents of the town
were up and about shopping and chatting; carrying bulging bags of
fruit and vegetables. We also noticed the stripped down wire shopping
baskets in use. The racing shopping trolleys as we christened them.
We aimed the hire car up the hill to the village. Minutes later as we
entered the village we recognised the familiar smiling face of Maria,
the kefanion owner- laden with bags of fruit. We waved and parked the
car a 100 yards further on, near the church. Maria caught us up and
we offered her our help with her shopping. Before she accepted one
bag was opened and we were handed a fresh apricot each. We were up
early she observed. We explained about Manos, the planner and the
house using our usual communication medium of signs, English and
smatterings of greek words – I think she understood. The shopping
was dropped off at the blue door of her kefanion and we said our
goodbyes and went down the steps to our house.

Cocks were crowing and there were signs of the village waking up with
doors open and pools of water by the clay pots and climbers in the
narrow village alleyways. Some furtive cats stalked past, still with their
night-hunting eyes before their sleep for the day.

We opened up the door and shutters allowing the strong morning light
and heat to enter the building. Looking around we hoped that the
house would impress the planner with it's potential as it had already
on us and Manos. Shortly before 8 my phone rang – "Hi, glad I have
caught you –where are you?"

I explained that we were at the house for the meeting scheduled,
checking my watch, in three minutes time. "Oh shit " said Manos –
clearly working to a more relaxed time regime –"I thought I would
catch you- he can't come this morning – there is a crisis with the plan-

ning consents for the town police station." As excuses went it was a good one.

"I will reschedule with him but it may be after you have returned to England.

I will see you later. "

We hid our disappointment –looked around the house –this wasn't proving to be plain sailing. We headed down the hill for a consolatory breakfast –still the sun was shining and permission had not been rejected –yet.

This holiday had a different character to previous ones. Local friends in the town now had different conversations with us. Did we know about the new builders merchant or tile shop outside the next town?" "You must be sure to be here at Easter, or the church saint's day." It was also said that we must visit outside the normal season when friends with businesses serving tourists would be free to meet for meals and drinks. Friends also felt we should be appraised of any decorative or architectural developments on the island. They would ask whether we had been to this or that new shop, or seen the new ceiling in this or that bar of restaurant –it was very helpful. Such recommendations had additional benefits. George's girlfriend suggested we looked at the furniture and décor in a new café bar opened by someone she knew. It was only a short walk along the coast from the town centre and had the benefit of a pool available to customers. It was interesting for us because the owners had re-used old weathered doors and shutters in the lovely aged Mediterranean paint colours. These were being recycled as table and counter tops after having sheets of plate glass placed on top. The matching turquoise and blue soft furnishing had also been sourced locally. Over drinks and a welcome lunch we complimented the owner on the "look" that had been created further chat revealed he was also restoring a house in the same hill village and knew our architect. He invited us to view his house and after brief directions he said cryptically "don't worry – you will know when you have found it – there are some unique features. Go in, just remove the bedstead that I am using as a gate!"

The next day whilst up at the house again, this time looking at our collection of old doors and shutters and imagining new creative uses for them we remembered his directions. We followed them, not without difficulty, the village was a rabbit warren of narrow streets and alleyways. Finding an old metal bedstead and moving to one side we were suddenly certain that we had found the house. The house, which was a typical building site with new stonework and also piles of rubble, had the most amazing ceiling. The whole of the ceiling was covered in ir-regular bleached rough branches, the effect was like a ceiling made of bones or antlers – it was amazing! The contrast with the grey almost regular stonework was stark –we were impressed and said so when we returned to the café later. "Good luck with your house – let me know if you need to know where to get anything." It seemed a typical reaction to our renovating a house – we had yet to encounter any resentment over foreign or second home ownership.

Our visits to towns and villages also saw us taking greater interest in windows and shutters, balconies and roof styles. There were shops that we had previously ignored that we now eagerly peered through the windows when closed or cautiously wandered around if open. All the time thinking that knowledge of the greek for "just looking" would be helpful.

Heraklion

Before we returned to England we had arranged to meet Manos in the capital, Heraklion, where he was to "escape" from his conference. There was a drive of about an hour and we gratefully parked the hire car near the bus station below the high stone city walls. It was only 10 a.m. but already very hot. We sat in the shade drinking iced coffees watching out for Manos. We only just spotted him. To our surprise the conference dress code seemed to be "urban guerrilla" as he was wearing the obligatory dark shades below a forage cap, T shirt and combat boots and trousers, all in camouflage khaki and green. All his possessions, phone, PDA, wallet , cigarettes etc were in the dozen or so pockets in the trousers making him clank and rattle as he walked. No matter we were pleased to see one another and he led us to where his Jeep was parked – in the bus station! 'Do you know your way around the city? No matter – the traffic is a bit chaotic. I will show you a few interesting places." He then steered us through the increasingly random streams of traffic; not allowing conversation to distract him from lighting and smoking his cigarette interrupted by several phone calls, naturally conducted in rapid greek at high volume. After several minutes drive along the coast we parked inside a stone mason's yard were we were invited to inspect different types of marbles and other types of stones with an explanation from Manos that they were very skilled here- able to create al sorts of things in stone- sinks, work-tops, tables etc. He left some papers with them that comprised some material orders and we set off again in the car. A few minutes later we drew up outside another yard that he explained was the only architectural recovery company that existed on the island. There wasn't time to look around but we now knew where it was; we completed a dramatic u-turn in a cloud of dust and momentarily concentrating on driving and not distracted by phone calls or smoking we burst out of the side road back into the hurly-burly of the city's traffic. We seemed to pass right through the centre and started climbing up on a road which had been entirely stripped of it's tarmac surface. This was where we would find electrical, furniture and bathroom stores and a few were pointed out to us. We carried on driving south through the suburbs until we were in a lush, green valley with an ancient aquaduct bisecting it. Manos pointed out a house on a hill above us that he had designed some years before – we stopped and he took some photos. Then swiftly executing another dusty u-turn he announced that he had better return to the conference and would drop us back at our car park.

Back in the city we waved him off and braced ourselves to drive back through the city centre, this time with me driving. The unmade main road shook the whole of the little hire car and great clouds of dust obscured much of the road ahead. By some miracle we found ourselves back in the area that Manos had recently shown us but on parking realised something of a flaw in the plan. The scraping away of the surface had resulted in the pavement in front of the shops being some two to three feet above the road surface. To clamber up required going on all fours in the dust.

This placed a limitation on our "shopping" as S. not unreasonably, announced she was only going to shops she could arrive at in the vertical position and preferably with a minimum covering of dust. In the event even the shops we could get to were irrelevant to us at this stage of the project and the only useful new shop we found was a hand-made glass lamp shade shop. The lights were very individual and the owners said that bespoke shapes and colours were also possible. We mentally tucked the place away for the future – if we could ever find it again!

Living Small

One of the things that had first attracted us to the house was starting to present us with some interesting questions. It was all really about space; or more correctly, the lack of it. There had been consideration of the size of the house before but this had been quickly dismissed with talk of "we are on holiday in a warm climate- not may clothes are needed –eating out is cheap, life here should be simpler than at home –not lots of possessions –no room!

But when planning the actual use of the space there was no getting away from the physical dimensions –two rooms, one above the other that were approximately four metres square, that's around 15 feet! The real challenge was installing the necessities of modern life and it really was a blank sheet of paper as to where we would put them. We were also not short of advice. Maria at the apartment that we rented had a preference for the bedroom downstairs – "it will be cooler" This cause a slight dilemma as space constraints rather suggested a bed-sitting room which we would prefer upstairs. Manos also favoured the plumbing for the bathroom on the ground floor which was pointing to-wards a hall, kitchen, bathroom combination, There was debate with others over the ideal location for the kitchen – where would we be eat-ing most frequently – on the yet to be approved sun-terrace?
The terrace was the subject of much discussion itself. We were con-cerned that this needed a building permit i.e. planning permission and we wanted reassurance that this would be granted. Manos in the local café bar insisted this would be our most used living space and certain-ly the potential view would be spectacular. As long as it was large enough for a table and seats for four or five friends it would be ideal.

The whole process of planning space in the house was going to be dominated by the small size of the house. In the early stages it did seem like an exercise on a (small) blank sheet of paper. There were no services in the house and the position of the stairs could be altered. We were going to adapt the old roof and possibly the roof-line to allow a new roof terrace The ground floor would be excavated for the drains and we had relative freedom over where to put sinks and taps etc – even which floor (from a choice of two!) we would put the kitchen or bathroom on.

One of our preoccupations was the question of the sea view. This was only clearly visible from what was a blank wall on the left hand side of the house; this wall had no openings at all at present and abutted a neighbours yard. At present by leaning out of the longer window, a form of french doors in the first floor the sea view could be glimpsed so a small balcony was another option but the street or in truth the alleyway in front of the house was less than two metres wide and the view would be limited.

The favoured option was to make some opening above to either a flat roof or some form of roof terrace at roof level.

The access up to this area would present us with further issues of space management in placing a second staircase into an area where we were already struggling for space for a bathroom and a kitchen. We tried to get some clear thinking on what needed to be fixed and what could be more flexible and to help with this we drew up a series of options for each floor – listing the advantages and disadvantages of the different layouts.

In all the alternatives we had assumed a roof terrace with the necessary access from inside the house on the first floor.

The first option would have a ground floor Hall, with table and chairs and a Kitchen. The first floor room would have bedroom and sitting as well as the bathroom.

The advantages of this option are more space for bed/sitting, bathroom near the bedroom, kitchen diner when not using the roof terrace, bedroom not "on the street" , table and chairs handy for the street.

The disadvantages are the bathroom in the sitting room and two sets of stairs to the terrace from the kitchen.

The second option was to use the ground floor for a Hall, winter Dining and Bathroom. The first floor room would combine a Bed/Sitting room with the Kitchen.

The advantages with this option are Bedroom "not on the street" and Bathroom away from the Sitting area but the disadvantages are cooking smells in the bedroom and two sets of stairs between terrace and the Bathroom.

The third option was to place a bedroom and bathroom on the ground floor and Sitting, Dining and Kitchen on the first floor. Advantages were the separation of living and sleeping space but the disadvantages were the lack of bed-sitting options.

There were at least two other less conventional options .One would be to put the bedroom and sitting on the ground floor with the kitchen and bathroom both on the first floor. The ground floor would be the darker room and it would definitely be a disadvantage for the living area to be there; although until cooling and heating were decided on it would be likely that the lower room would always be cooler.

The second would be to combine a bedroom and kitchen on the ground floor with the bathroom and sitting area upstairs but that just felt wrong for a number of reasons.

God this was proving to be quite difficult!

I think this was so for a number of reasons

Firstly, there was our relative ignorance of living and planning a house for living in a Mediterranean climate.

We had planned and extended and adapted houses at home but the process seemed much harder for this house.

We had holidayed here – at the height of summer and in the spring and autumn but longer periods here would be different- there would be more eating at home, less going out and more home based activities. We planned to indulge in hobbies, painting, photography, writing. We wanted to entertain so would need to be able to cook and serve food albeit to small groups of people. The apartments and small villas we had stayed in were very different to this house and we had used them differently so there was a certain amount of "imagineering" as to what our lives as home owners on the island would be like and what we would need from the house to live this life.

Then there was the restriction of space –there was no escaping the fact it was a tiny house.

Next Autumn Visit

This autumn visit started in a more than usually chaotic fashion when we arrived at the airport and smugly breezed through carrying hand luggage to find that our hire car was not at the airport. After a phone call to the office we were promised delivery in half an hour. We knew the journey always took us almost an hour so were surprised to see the car arrive forty minutes later. I felt the engine must be red-hot so drove it back at "normal" speed whilst getting used to the Cretan traffic. It was late afternoon so we were able to collect some bags of clothes left at a friend's shop at the end of the last visit. After dropping the bags at the apartment and a quick shower we were out again for an evening meal. The first day or two of any visit were always punctuated by renewing acquaintances and catching up on friends news. Also fielding enquiries about progress on the house –" Do you have the permit yet? When will work start –soon ? Accompanied by stories of other building projects and their progress – or lack of it !
All of this would be carried out sitting in the sun or the warmth of the evening enjoying good food or cold drinks.

During the autumn visit to the island we were hopeful of finally receiving the necessary planning consents – the building permit.
The first visit to the architect was not a success, at least as far as pushing progress. Just as we had finished exchanging pleasantries and were getting down to some serious discussion about the building permit the office degenerated into chaos. The full complement of day time staff returned with two strangers who we were introduced to – these are other clients with a house in Kritsa, we are all off to the opening of their photographic exhibition – you must come along ….we are going now. We really had no choice and with initial reluctance we tagged along. The exhibition was in a series of large upstairs rooms in an old, rather grand building overlooking one of main streets leading down to the harbour. The rooms were already crowded with people drinking wine and chatting with some of the crowd having spilt out onto the large balcony overlooking the street – a table at the end of one of the rooms creaked under large plates of food.
I noticed that the reason we were all there were visibly hanging on the wall – a number of beautiful framed photographs of scenes on Crete, portraits, old buildings, architectural details. There was a call for quiet,

several I think as Greek crowds love to talk! Finally a distinguished gent spoke at length in Greek. After the applause had died down there was an edited translation in English. The gist of which was that Phil had been traveling to the island for a number of years and now had a holiday home in one of the hill villages. Someone in the town chamber of commerce had seen his photos posted on the internet and asked him if he would be interested in an exhibition of his work in the town gallery. The rest was history!

We joined the other visitors in more drinks and "eats. "It was turning into a good evening.

We were introduced again to the photographer and found we had un-beknown to them been shown around their house as a work in progress by our mutual architect. This was a first for me – being intro-duced for the first time to someone who's house I had already visited! The conversation was reassuring –they were very happy with their house the works were of good quality and "worth waiting for" – those last words were to gain greater significance to us in the future.

We completed the evening by buying one of the beautiful framed pho-tos. The whole event had been so typical of a spontaneous evening on the island.

On the next visit to the office we were introduced to a new face –'this is Marina, a recent architecture graduate and the daughter of a friend of mine. I would like her to give some fresh thought to the house inte-rior and together we will all put forward some new ideas; talk together and discuss your requirements.' This was a new approach. To date Manos had been almost possessive about the various options we had been discussing together. Still it was a welcome distraction from the matter of the outstanding building permit.

Marina was very pleasant, with fluent English, naturally.

We had a useful and fairly freewheeling discussion that concluded with Marina suggesting that it sounded like we were looking for a studio/ work space that we could also holiday in –combining creative activities with holidays in the sun. This was very perceptive of her and summed up our requirements quite accurately and took us beyond some of the nitty gritty requirements of drains and bathrooms. The downside was this was also placing further demands on somewhere we had already considered as a very small space. Nevertheless, the conclusion was that all four of us would over the next few weeks come up with some proposals for the two rooms. An arbitrary date, some five weeks in the future was plucked out of the air by Manos – this would be the deadline for everyone's plans!

We spent some time this holiday just sitting up at the house; soaking in the atmosphere and trying to visualize how it could be sympathetically renovated. On our last visit we had seen some interesting recycling of old shutters as new tables and we looked at our "store" of house contents with new interest. It was also pleasing to see that the thick stone walls and small windows coupled with the position of the village provided some natural cooling even in the heat of the day.

Another House

Before we flew home we had arranged to meet Manos for supper and he said we should eat in a new restaurant in one of the hill villages. When we arrived there he proposed showing us a house that had recently been taken onto their books with a view to restoration as a sort of "show home." He explained the elderly owner through ill-health had to leave in a hurry and they had decided to buy the house to provide her with a quick sale. We were intrigued and we were not to know, at this stage, what part this house would play in our future.

Arriving in the village we turned down a series of winding streets to park opposite what appeared to be a bridge over a deep concreted storm drain – almost a drained canal.

The visit was made by torchlight to what was, in truth, an embryonic building site. There were piles of clay bricks, bags of cement , a cement mixer and reels of reinforcing wire but there was work-in-progress. Manos outlined his plans for a small wet-room, galley kitchen, a study area, and a new staircase to a small first floor bedroom. New walls were being built to reconfigure the ground floor to get a better designed layout, though in the present state it was very difficult to imagine what the finished layout would be and viewing by torchlight didn't help. From what would become a small first floor bedroom was a doorway out to a large roof terrace in the process of construction on the flat roof of the house. There was plenty of space up here and plans were explained by Manos for outside dining a sink and barbeque area, a chimney for a woodstove to be installed downstairs and of room for services such as air-con units and a satellite dish! The view was also described as very scenic but apart from a few other house lights and one or two dim street lights this was difficult to confirm.

It gave us some confidence because although we had viewed some completed or near completed projects this was far and away more dramatic in terms of work required and at that stage we assumed our own house was in better order and needing less extensive building works The evening ended socially with a meal, outdoors in a nearby village restaurant, freshly cooked local dishes or a variety of mezes with chilled local wine all consumed under a spreading tree full of singing crickets. Coincidentally we also met for the second time one of Manos's previous customers whose own house was around the corner and we were reminded that we had been shown around it in it's almost completed state shortly after we had bought our own house.

Once back home we used our time as a continuation of what we had been doing since we had first seen the house. Magazines were browsed, architecture and interior style books were collected from the library or bought in bookshops and from Amazon. Television house building and renovation programmes were watched for inspiration. It was truly exciting for us to be planning a home from scratch albeit one with no services, currently and two windows and one door! The phrase "living small" had never sounded more accurate. Some of the books and magazines were helpful and we liked some of the more playful and imaginative ideas. Our original ideas had been based on small spaces we were aware of – studio flats, beach huts, camper vans and cara-vans. The idea of convertible furniture and slide away surface and doors – we even found a picture of a ladder style stairs that slid out of a bookcase/storage wall. Given that the in the house there was already a loft hatch at the top of the stairs that folded down and covered the stair well, presumably to give more space upstairs; some of these ideas did not seem so radical or unsympathetic to the original house design.

During this time official confirmation of the Building Permit was re-ceived – and we were now known to the police !

I am very pleased to tell you that we now have the Building Permit.
I will send you another email informing you about the money to send related to the Building Permit.
We have already informed the Police Station in Elounda and are bringing to them a copy of the Building Permit.
We have located the number of the Building Permit on the property Door
M.

We drafted our ideas in a series of floor plans and drawings complete with an explanatory narrative. We had settled on a kitchen area on the left hand side of the ground floor with a bathroom also located on that level, using the space under the stairs. The first floor was seen as a 'studio' space combining small work areas for the both pf us with a Bed-sitting area. We also proposed using niche areas throughout the house for storage and open display areas, these were the details that we mailed him:-

Niches

1. small niches as hand-holds instead of a hand rail- at hand height as you climb. These could also be on the second stairs depending on their construction.

2. A full-length niche inside the door on the ground floor front wall to use as fold down table for a dining area using old wood with a cupboard below.

3. A back wall niche to create space in both the kitchen and bathroom-it could be two niches. We like the idea of a 'gash' of glass across the back wall – bringing light in during the day – could be lit by coloured lights in the night.

4. The Kitchen niche – a long one, if possible, to echo the run of the work surface and to provide a decorative storage area.

5. A study niche on the first floor – we thought two small study areas/desks split by a tall wardrobe cupboard.

6. A niche at the foot of the second staircase (as large as possible as a cupboard.)

7. First floor – a second mid-height niche to match the existing one in the middle of the left hand side-wall.r

List of things to keep from the house:-

Pithori
Old shutters (3)
Wooden boxes

Staircase
Stairs hatch
Round stone
Front door
Pair of green shutters
Single shutter
Anything else you think could be useful

Please call/email if anything is unclear
our best regards and thanks
Geoff

Looking at Plans

When Marina's ideas arrived they were interesting . I quote from some of the text: "the idea of the house is that it looks like a cave. The ground floor is very dark. The external walls are from stones and the additional parts that contain the kitchen, bathroom and the bed are built in with concrete walls in organic form. The sliding doors covering these can be painted and hung with canvases, like a gallery."
A curved wooden staircase was shown up to the first floor with the wall beside it containing many little niches with hidden lights. "leading out of the cave up to more natural light upstairs that would be a studio/ work room." There were also some very clever ideas picking up on our brief of multifunctional use and inspirations that we had discussed from caravan or boat interiors with folding tables and benches.
Her stairs were shown as a curving staircase and she was also proposing the ground floor to have some "living room" features as well as serving as a kitchen.
We conclude that our own ideas had been relatively safe and angular in design; we couldn't wait to see what Manos would come up with.
In the event it was several weeks after the deadline that he himself had chosen, that the first set of ideas from Manos arrived.
But they were worth the wait. The plan itself was a single sheet of paper with a floor plan and elevations sketched as little coloured drawings. The notation was so small on the original A4 that we could only read it after I had enlarged it on our printer!
The plan also contained a series of messages to us, I quote :-

"I have elaborated a lot of other solutions but all seem to me very artificial, boxy, claustrophobic. This one is probably the only one with almost full open plan room with light and a social area

So, colours and materials: white stone as you indicated for the floor. Eventually, (visible iron beams for ceiling) rusted – niches in stone and pointed, rest of the walls pressed (?) plaster plus old wooden planks and a lot of glass / plexiglass and colour.
All niches are in visible, pointed stone. All niches have interior lights, any shelves are glass or plexiglass, some coloured. "
The plan itself showed a wet room to the right of the front door with a

staircase over which started on the back wall and turned ninety degrees to climb over the wetroom. The bottom half of the stairs before it tuned were behind a floor to ceiling glass slate. There were niches on the other three walls. The left hand side of the room was split between storage/ seating at the back with a kitchen area next to the new window on front wall. A glass or stone slab was drawn as a curving work surface which split the room and had stools under. A new small window was drawn in on the front wall to ventilate and light the wet room.

 A lot seemed to have been fitted in but we liked a number of the ideas and it seemed to make sense to have a ground floor "social" area as long as there was enough room. We were so excited that we overlooked the lack of a plan for the first floor ; this was to follow a while later. In the meantime we sent some comments on the plan, this was the way we worked through the project, as a dialogue. Sometimes it felt that we were in tune with each other; at other times there was a lot more work required to evolve a joint solution.

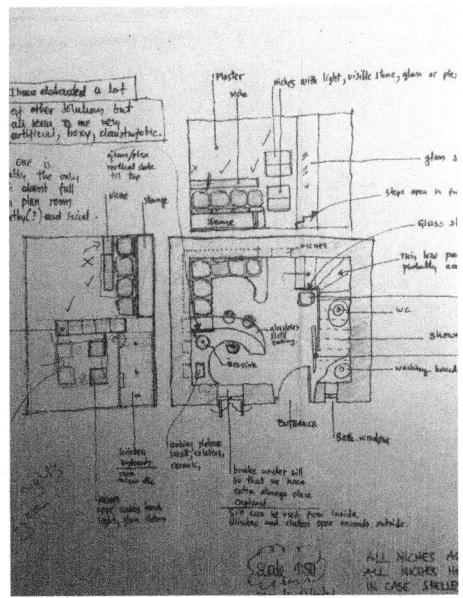

Our first comments on ground floor were:

1. We like very much the design for the kitchen area

with the separate 'social seating and breakfast bar'

2. Kitchen – we like it but we will need to ensure that sufficient storage and space for fridge, micro-wave /oven combination etc.

3. Social seating – perhaps this could be combined with Marina's idea for an occasional bed.

4. Stairs –this seems a good position and divides the bathroom from the kitchen/social area. We like the glass wall 'slate to top' idea. We wonder if Marina's myriad of lit niches could be incorporated up the stairs to light the way –this would be gorgeous.

5. Bathroom – the position on this wall is a good solution – reasons: separate from kitchen/living; more space freed up; more privacy/light & ventilation possible there.

6. Front door –Marina drew in a double door which seemed good and space saving-it looked like a traditional design too?

7. Any thoughts about the back wall niche as a 'gash of light' and whether glass bricks are an option for this here or upstairs?

Upstairs –we have already sent some of our ideas but we are still unsure of the best position for access to the roof terrace and this will decide the stairs position.

We sent a picture of a clever slide out stairs that we found and his could perhaps be possible. Marina's positioning of the stairs in the lower part of the ceiling makes some sense.

We see the first floor as lighter – able to get some air in through the French doors/ small balcony and roof access.

Purpose of the room – sleeping/seating, entertaining, study and storage- quite a challenge!

We think it's going to be really good and are very excited about the whole project.

We had some further conversation and after some thought we sent more comments:

"We have some views on the overall colour scheme.
We really liked the tiny details you added to the house in Kritsa –using coloured tiles. We don't want to restrict your palette but would like something similar using plain/etched/textured/patterned glass, using occasional details in textured, translucent or metallic mosaic tiles – in natural /neutral white-cream-light or dark grey/Inox or shell/stone rather than bright colours.
This is because we like to change the colours in our home and if a definite colour is used on a fixed object-say work/floor/tiled surface we are likely to get bored with it and want to change it. Also a more neutral palette gives us more options for adding a wider range of colour. We can add colour with furnishing fabric/ household objects /lights/ornaments/accessories and these can be changed as and when we want to – but create the interest in more permanent features by limited colour but interesting textures and finishes.
We are not asking for bland – this will give you loads of scope to create something beautiful.

So that floor surfaces , shelves, glass, work tops and tiling will be light, neutral colours with accessories using brighter colours that can be changed when required against the neutral backdrop of the house.

Finishes:
Although much of the house will have a modern look with glass, modern materials and lighting we talked of using some of the old wood from the house perhaps as cupboard doors to use some of the previous history of the house. This could be stained of colour washed or varnished over the bleached paint.

Lighting and power –this needs to be sufficient and flexible for living/ working and to zone areas e.g. the kitchen/ ground floor social area. Where feasible energy efficient low wattage or LED's to be used.

Ground Floor

- One of Marina's plans showed a double front door which would be space saving within the thickness of the exterior walls.

123

- The new high-level window for the bathroom could be constructed to include a shelf and some other storage is needed in the bathroom perhaps in a niche or under the sink.
- Ground floor windows- privacy should be maintained by use of mirrored glass.
- Kitchen work-surface-sufficient overhang should exist to avoid any diagonal lines being visible from appliances or storage below.
- The new metallic pole to support the glass staircase could be utilised for a 'clamp on' organic shaped curved table top that could be raised up to the ceiling and incorporating 12 volt stepped down powered lighting unit.
- The social seating area to be cut back on the right hand side to give clearer access and be level with the staircase glass (see plan)
- The storage under this seating will be most useful.
- Back wall niche to incorporate a row of glass bricks, neutral frosted.

First floor
- Lit niches on the right-hand side wall up the stairs.
- In the front wall a long cupboard niche to be created with doors for storage-doors in recovered wood.
- The full glass top to roof shelves to be created out of glass (not coloured)
- Back wall wardrobe storage to include drop down work surfaces for use at sitting height as desks. Two double sockets within at work surface height.
- Bed sofa to be either bought or constructed and will be against front or left hand side wall leaving a clear view of the glass stair well.

Sun Terrace
- Sink for washing with taps on the top sun terrace- could be on the floor in top right hand corner.
- Windows into the first floor room from the sun terrace.

The plan for the first floor, when it arrived, echoed some of the features of the ground floor plans: the stone wall niches with lights, the use of structural iron bars and glass. The most interesting feature was a proposal for a glass panel to the ground floor below a spiral staircase attached to a metal pole that went down through the building to the back, left hand side of the ground floor seating area . The spiral would go up to the new roof terrace. The spiral staircase was described as a "Light Well" topped by a glass roof hatch; this would bring light down through the building.

One night a short time late my mobile rang - Hello, are you at home ? Yes - why? It was Manos !
I will be sending you a fax - I have changed the plans .... new ideas...you will see... ring me when it arrives ...I hope you like it ....we will talk later...
cooking the evening meal was put on hold - the inbox was scanned for a fax notification and after a short wrestle with the laptop a four page fax was printed.
New ideas -certainly ! The roof terrace was to have a glass floor to go with the glass hatch and glass spiral staircase. Further close examination of the plans revealed a partial glass floor in the first floor room as well - the plan was annotated with "to bring light to the ground floor' The spiral stairs had been moved to a different corner of the building but it made more sense there. It would be amazing but was there a sudden glut of plate glass in Crete?
There would certainly be light but would the heat be a problem?
It was to be discussed.
We called back. We love it - "good but you need to think about it - and the colour. Here is a web site link you will see examples there and glass blocks they can be used on the terrace walls - the colours could be interesting. Let me know what you think of the colours - we are now blocked until you speak to me. We will proceed with other parts of the plan-the niches etc.
Now -do you know about cumquats. We answered "Yes" -nervously. Why- can you can make marmalade or confiture with cumquats -I have many of them outside my window. The conversation was taking a Cretan turn. There was much to consider - even before the question of cumquat chutney.
We eventually recommended using a bottling of the surplus-perhaps in brandy or metaxa -"Have you tried this ?" well No -we don't exactly get snowed under with cumquats in Sussex -or metaxa - " we have talked enough" the phone went dead - still it felt like progress -of sorts.

Next Spring Visit

The first visit of this year was an opportunity to stay in a house that had already been renovated . Impressively this was the one we had visited by torchlight only six months previously. We arranged to meet with Manos in a café near the office in the port and after a daytime flight we found ourselves in a café above the new marina enjoying a very welcome cooling drink. He arrived late and flustered and welcome us with a flurry of sorries and a bristly double cheek kiss each. 'Oh, it has been hectic in the office today...' –less hectic I quietly (and unkind- ly), thought to myself, now you are here and not still there. We had some more drinks and after Manos had relaxed and briefly discussed some of his plans for our house it was agreed we would follow him in our hire car up to the renovated house in the hills.

It was just as well that we did. We had previously been driven there in the dark and I doubt that I would have found it again in the rabbit warren of streets and alleyways. Eventually we drew up at the side of a large storm drain and after parking the cars crossed over it on a track. To our right at the end of a small street was a smart new green- stained wooden front door, set into a newly pointed stone wall with a newly plastered wall over it. "This is the house – come in" said Manos unlocking the door. We had only seen the house once, before the reno- vation works, in the dark, by torchlight. There had been a transforma- tion: the inside was bright and airy, a mix of plastered and original stone walls. There were lots of modern lights, a fitted kitchen and in- teresting objects and furniture. Manos opened the fridge and took out a bottle of wine and opening it said "please make yourselves at home here. Use the food and drink- they are for you and let me know of any- thing that is missing for comfortable living. You are the first people to stay here - it will be useful to you in finalising the detailed plans for your house." We looked around with him – it was such a transforma- tion and the layout was so interesting. On the ground-floor was one long room with a glass door at each end, screened by a translucent curtain. At one end was a comfortable sitting area with a large coloured sofa bed next to a coffee table and a corner fire place with a plastered chimney up to the ceiling. At the other end of the room was a fitted kitchen with all the necessary appliances as well as a small dining table cleverly fitted into an alcove. A vertical slice of glass gave a glimpse of a small desk and storage area below the stairs. These

were off to the left of the main room and ran up past a beautiful exposed stone wall.

There was only one room on the first floor – the bedroom but there was a useful fitted wardrobe, interesting small windows with shutters in green stained wood to match the front door and best of all a door out onto a large roof terrace. This was a great space with plenty of stone seating, or lying down space a dining table under a shady pergola made of old olive wood and thick canes for the roof. There was also a tap and large old stone sink, next to a barbecue area. There were views over the village , neighbouring gardens, the olive groves and the mountains – even a glimpse in the distance of the sea. We thought it was perfect and told Manos so – he was suitably modest and said that it was a rush job, achieved cheaply. We were not entirely convinced – there seemed good quality fittings and attention to detail in the finish but we found this reassuring.

The house lacked for nothing in terms of amenities, there were two air-conditioning units, a power shower, oven, hob, washing machine, satellite tv, dvd and stereo – a real home from home, with better weather! We were very impressed and grateful to Manos – our frustration at the slow start for our house evaporated – at least for the time being.

By staying in the Kritsa house we placed some distance between the house renovation project and us; it meant we could treat the stay as more of a holiday. The downside was that any site visits to the house meant a twenty mile round trip but at least we could separate ourselves from the slow progress on renovation. The benefits included experiencing life in a greek house in a village and living in a new place. Our stay in the house as the first residents since the rebuild led to a misunderstanding. This took place the second afternoon of our stay.

We were locking the front door to take a stroll up into the village for a coffee or a cold drink when we were hailed from the garden next door. An elderly smiling man was calling to use from his chair at a table on a shady terrace behind the house next door. We replied good afternoon in our best greek but he indicated that we should come into his garden and sit down. It seemed only polite to comply and to explain we were going out and our greek might make conversation tricky was a more difficult option. We sat down and all smiled at each other. Names were exchanged – he was called Michalis – and he pushed some of the walnuts he was cracking open towards us. Smiling he showed us that the nuts were ripe enough to be cracked open using bare hands. The brief conversation was punctuated by a chorus of barking from a small dog tethered to a kennel in a separate fenced off part of the shady garden. We were asked if we like the nuts and replied in broken greek with a question whether they were from the garden. This was met with laughter - "No, No – from Katharo " this was a plateau higher up in the mountains that we knew was heavily cultivated with products beyond the ubiquitous olive tree. The walnuts or as we now learnt "krimithia" were delicious. Unfortunately, their dryness started me coughing. "Eleni!" called Michaelis with a surprisingly loud voice.

We heard some noise from behind a curtain over the door and a very small lady wearing an apron, her silver hair pinned up in a bun, appeared from inside the house. She was introduced as Eleni his wife and quickly was instructed to bring us drinks. Raki (the grape brandy) for me with fresh orange juice provided for ladies. When I questioned whether Michealis was drinking Raki he indicated a heart condition with cardia the greek for heart giving us 'cardiac' in English. We sat there, the three of us smiling at one another with the diminutive Eleni at a similar height although she was still standing. I offered her my seat but Michaelis quickly directed her into the house. Minutes later she appeared with a plate of peeled and sliced apple. This was followed by a plate of peeled pear. At last Eleni produced a tiny child sized chair from behind the curtain and sat down. It was time for a conversation that we would have to get used to in Crete – one of the first questions a greek asks you is "how old are you" usually quickly followed by their age and questions and statements about children and grand children. After we owned up about our ages we were informed that Michaelis was eighty two and Eleni was ninety two. We were dining with the oldest waitress and her toy boy that we had encountered so far on the island. The combined effect of the unaccustomed heat admittedly tempered by the shade of the garden; the afternoon raki and the stress of greek conversation meant that we would need to make our excuses and leave. We achieved this only after accepting a large bag of walnuts and pears. Putting those inside the front door we continued our stroll into town. This would not be our last conversation in the neighbour's garden.

The hill village was a tourist destination during the day with both cars and coaches bringing visitors to the long winding high street with a collection of cafes, tavernas and craft shops. Lace, leather, pottery and glassware as well as carved olive wood filled shops and spilled onto tables on the narrow pavement. In previous visits we had called there for a drink or a meal, sometimes en route to the higher Katharo plateau now known to us as the source of Michaelis's walnuts.

In the centre of the village was a small square where were a number of bars and tavernas shared the space and had placed their tables and chairs. We stopped for an iced coffee and reflected on the generous hospitality we had received from our new neighbours. We also speculated whether we would always be 'ambushed' when leaving the house – I couldn't be spending every outing in a

'raki haze' pleasant as it was. Although the days were often spent visiting the house project and driving out of the village on sorties to our favourite island spots most evenings found us back in the village. We mixed our time between using the kitchen at home to rustle up some cretan cuisine and eating suppers out in the village. In any event most evenings when there we walked round the village for a stroll. The place took on a different character at night. Most of the tourist craft shops were shut but the local food stores, bakers, butchers, hairdressers, ironmongers as well as the cafes and tavernas reopened for evening business; sometimes until a surprisingly late hour. This made the large village quite a buzzing place at night and as we became more recognised through the frequency of our strolls it was apparent that we had not just driven to the village for a "one-off" supper. Quite often we were politely asked where we were staying – not an unreasonable request as we had only spotted a couple of small buildings with 'rooms to rent' signs. The village, some 20 minute drive from the coast was more of a day trip destination. In the evenings we recognised the same people sitting outside their houses and the casual "kalinithkas" developed into longer conversations. By the end of the week we were chatting about our plans for our house, their children, culinary recommendations, the changes on the island – it was a very pleasant experience and something we looked forward to. There was the attendant benefit of being donated fruits and vegetables – "you must try our apricots from our garden – they are so good this season" We started to feel guilty – not having anything to offer in return but were assured by Manos when we discussed this dilemma with him that most families had some connection with tourism and just saw a collective benefit in our stay.

One morning there was a knock on the front door – S. opened it and for a split second thought that no-one was there, until looking down she saw all four foot six of Eleni looking up at her, smiling and holding a plateful of warm cheese pies as a gift. This was so kind... and they were delicious, melt in the mouth pastry covering warm feta cheese contrasting with a coating of sweet local honey! We called around later that day to take the neighbours some flowers as a thank you for the gift and their earlier hospitality to us. There was some stilted conversation (by us due to our limited greek) but it appeared that we should stay as Michaelis wanted us to meet someone. A few minutes later a smiling young lady carrying a gift wrapped box came into the garden. The mystery was soon cleared up – this was their grand daughter and much to our relief spoke fluent English – she worked as a secondary school teacher in the next town. Katerina had been phoned to be told about her grandparents new neighbours and asked to come and translate conversation. Drinks and plates were brought and the box of cakes was opened. "My grandparents are very pleased to have you as their new neighbours and hope you will be very happy in your new house." We thanked her but explained that we were only "borrowing" the house for stays whilst our house renovation in another village was being arranged and the house belonged to the architect. This comment was met with confused looks and an exchange in greek between our hosts and Katerina – they are sorry – they thought you had bought the house – my grandfather wants to know which village you prefer. I replied that we both liked his village very much – "Then he asks why have you bought a house in another village!" This was not going to be easy.

The Cost schedule – and a shock!

After some wait it arrived – the email with the promised schedule of costs – and it was a shock.

We had discussed different components and had, in the early stages, been given rough costings for the essential works.

The final figure was a consolidated total which could be described as a total "turn-key' cost with the schedule to include final cleaning and site clearance, painting and decorating and making some bespoke furniture that we had discussed. But....it was too much !!

It felt like one of the low points of the whole project.

During the last visit to the island we had completed detailed plans even including where two-way light switches would be. The details also were an opportunity to properly consider how the necessary storage could be incorporated into the small areas that we were working with. Some of these plans were very creative and exciting and were a continuation of the periodic debate about our 'niches.' The incorporation of glass panels and built in storage was certainly a great way of making the most of the small, dark rooms but the reality of the cost of this bespoke design was a sobering wake up call.

For a few days we did nothing. We were shocked –it was much more than we were expecting and when we did talk about it we considered some extreme options which included valuing the house with the building permit and putting it up for sale. Another less radical option would be to put the renovation on hold and move in on a "camping" basis – using water from the village tap, solar, battery lights of a generator and awaiting the arrival of mains drainage, (an option already rumoured to be employed by an American owner living around the corner!)

Then we considered abandoning the architect and looking for other builders to quote –though how this practical this was from a distance of almost 2000 miles.

Thinking how we had got to this point we recalled so many discussions and options that had been thought of , refined or developed or ultimately discarded. Surely it wouldn't end with us selling it before we had ever stayed there?

At the first site meeting with Manos we had considered the roof terrace and small balcony. The lack of the view and difficulties in creating openings in order to achieve this. Later, when planning consents were being arranged there were the awkward dialogues with the planners when there was the need to convince them we weren't trying to create a third storey but only a small terrace to allow us to see the view. At that point we considered abandoning the terrace idea and constructing some bizarre 'viewing platform' in the corner of the first floor room and making a virtue out of this by placing much-needed storage underneath.

At this point I decided to contact someone we had met in one of the other villages whose house had already been renovated. This provided some welcome reassurances as their experience had been very similar. I was reassured that this "all in price" was certainly negotiable and it had, in all probability, been partially caused by all our "interesting' design additions. When they had similarly asked where costs could be reduced they had been told "everywhere!"

So the discussions began. It was right –the question was met with the same answer – "of course, everywhere." Certainly, any activity we would have carried out ourselves at home was to be excluded, so internal decorating was out. There was also the more "adventurous" elements which when suggested and the cost had been questioned were normally met with a "No, it would not be expensive!"

When all of these were added together – expense did seem an issue. The glass spiral stairs up to the terrace were questioned – Yes they would, in fact be more expensive than a more normal metal staircase. "Right, we will be having metal then."

At the end of some of these discussions we took stock with Manos –"the house will still be interesting with these changes?" –
"Of course"

"And we will still use some glass to get light down through the house ?"

-"Yes, that will still be done"

-"Ok then"

It was agreed that Manos would completely review the cost schedule with a view to removing optional costs as well as any costs for activities that we could do ourselves such as decorating. We had an anxious couple of weeks awaiting the new quotation wondering whether we would have to reconsider, mothball or even completely abandon the project. It was a real low point in the whole enterprise and to make things worse that summer was a particularly miserable one in Sussex

– cold and wet. The idea of a completed holiday home in the sun seemed particularly appealing but seemed a distant prospect.

A revised cost schedule arrived late that summer which certainly made a reduction to the total and several weeks of revisions followed back and forth between Crete and Sussex. It was agreed that the final draft would be signed when we returned for our autumn holiday in a few week's time.

Works to Start !!

The October trip had seen us staying in the renovated house in the hills again. The main house activity on this visit was the finalising of the works and project management contract.

Email drafts had been exchanged back and forth between Crete and Sussex the previous month and we really hoped to finalise details of costs and sign the contract.

The island was warm as usual for this time of year. The progress to this point had seemed slow with the delay on planning consents followed by the long discussions and email about how the house should be designed. The lack of space limited some options but also meant that more care was necessary with the limitations placed on us by this. Manos's office was again inspirational with the shelves full of architectural books and glass tables laden with glossy magazines.

One evening we were introduced to the idea of using a small mini digger to dig out the septic tank under the house and we were given an explanation of how access would be created by removing half of the front wall !! In short order we were introduced to the plant operator who had called into the office. He unsuccessfully tried to reassure us by showing a photo of his mini-digger on his phone while giving us vocal impressions of it. I must admit we were far from reassured!

Staying in the renovated house had a number of advantages for us. It allowed us to more carefully consider our real requirements for storage as well as day to day living in a warm climate.

The house had a number of features that we enjoyed and hoped could be incorporated into the design of our house.

There was a coolness in the downstairs room – helped by the small window, shutters and the ability to get a through draught – taking the warm air up the stairs and out onto the terrace.

The terrace itself provided both shade and sun and proved to be the place for breakfast under the shade and supper at sunset.

Colour in the house was generally limited to highlights with the background colour being lighter and cooler.

Lighting was flexible with feature lighting and useful dimmers.

High-level storage made the most of the space.

Sympathetic mixes of contrasting materials provided interest – glass, thick ply cut across the layers, exposed stone, limed wood and painted concrete, recycled old wood with faded paint, aged Olive wood beams.

These requirements were discussed at length both by ourselves and later with Manos in his office and more leisurely under the stars over supper on the terrace of one of the restaurants. Some decisions were made during these talks: the ground floor would have a stone floor as light coloured as possible and soft, irregular shaped tiles.
There wouldn't be a chimney or a wood stove – the space it would need could not be sacrificed. Seating areas were needed on all floors and should be combined with storage. – some could be fixed.
An emergency water tank was advised for when the mains supply was interrupted, this could be placed in the floor and linked to a pump.
Some supply of water would be useful to the roof terrace, a small sink perhaps.
Some screening on the terrace for shading and privacy was needed.
Various ways of bringing light into the ground floor was talked about; some glass panels in the floor was a possibility, bringing natural light down through the building.
A small safe should be provided with enough space for storing a laptop computer. Some of the old wood that had been saved from the house could be recycled and used as features.

The signing of the works contract itself was toasted in the office with glasses of champagne – the talking, planning and thinking phase was at last at an end – or at least we hoped it was !
The celebrations were indeed premature as can be seen from a few sample emails from Crete that were sent to us that winter.

November
Greetings to you both.
It is still raining here.   We need a two week period without any rain at all and it to be completely dry before we start demolishing, so that we do not have problems.
We will inform you when we can start.
Best wishes.
M

December passed and Christmas came and went in England and Crete; we seemed to have drifted into another period of inactivity on the project. We had agreed everything, signed the contracts and been told that the builders and specialists were ready and willing to start, eager even! It seemed ironic that wet weather in Crete was delaying things – England was sunny and cold. We awaited news.

17 january
Many greetings to you and I hope you are both well.
I am pleased to inform you that we are finally starting works on Wednesday next week, I will keep you informed.
Best wishes to you from a warm and sunny Crete.
Kind regards.
M.

Many greetings – thanks for the funds transfer.
The electrician started with the electric connection to the mains. As soon as we sign the connection contracts and have also electricity (the water is connected) we will start.
Finally, an email arrived on a sunny February morning in Sussex –

We have finally started.!
This the depth achieved after 30 hrs of digging.
The initial debris and stone has already been transported away and that is what we are doing every two days.
It is extremely hard.
I am attaching 7 photos and will keep updating you.
Best regards
M.

Attached to the email were indeed seven photos and as we said in our reply, seldom have any photos of rubble and a hole in the ground caused as much excitement, certainly outside the world of archeology, and definitely not in our house before!
The photos showed the impact that our small house renovation was having in the small village. The first photo was of the builders JCB style digger parked in the street above our house –it blocked the narrow street; just beyond it we caught a glimpse of Maria's kefenion. At

least we could hope that the disruption to her might be off-set by some extra business from thirsty and hungry builders. The second photo was of the alleyway in front of our house. A builder stood with his back to the camera –admiring his wheelbarrow, the ground in front of the house was a mix of red mud and piles of rocks- we could see the front door-way with a yellow hydraulic hose snaking down the alley-way and disappearing inside the house. Above the house seen below the end of the street was a blue glimpse of the sea.

The next few photos were more shocking but certainly demonstrated progress. The floor downstairs had all but disappeared. In it's place was a deep grey-white hole –it looked brown at the bottom- some random hydraulic 'jack-hammer' were scattered next to the hole offering some clues as to the creation of the hole. The hole looked five foot deep ! At last, the works had started and it looked as if there had been a rethink and it was being carried out without the partial demolition of the front for machine access. This was good news

We emailed back….

Thanks - seldom have two people been so excited about some rubble and a hole !!

We will call you again soon.

Thanks again

Hi there

Yesterday after your telephone call a lady lawyer living close has protested about the noise so we stopped to make her calm, to restart Monday. I am attaching 5 photos one of which is the small van this morning

Enjoy your Sunday
M.

17 Feb
Good Morning,
Here is snowing.
Yesterday we took away last debris.
Pit has reached its 2,50 m in deepness.
I have tried not to disturb the house physically and also the houses around all along the very narrow road.
If the small caterpillar would have entered this area as we were planning in order to contain cost, this almost ''surgery operation'' would have not happened.
We, of course, have harassed the village, and for an extended time, blocking completely the road for more than 10 hours per day and making too match noise but the blame after all is on me....
So, it seems that the most delicate and expensive phase is over. (I will gather costs and send them to you).
Now it's becoming a builders work.
In the mean time some things might change in relation of the extension and type of reinforcement , since the house is standing on an excellent extra solid rock foundation from what we have verified.
The water has been connected.

I am attaching 8 pictures taken on the 14th of February and 6 taken this morning.
I am pleased to inform you that everything has been organised for works to start on 26th March
M.

Well it was too good to resist – I would call him. After exchanging pleasantries and discussing the weather I was able to ask him what he thought about progress so far and also to probe further on the cryptic comment in the earlier email about "some things changing…..since the house is standing on an excellent extra solid rock foundation!!!!"

The last Saturday in March, the clocks go forward tonight, spring is here. The last email had stated that building works were to begin on

Wednesday 26th March–our expectations were not high for major progress for a few days yet.

Surprise…. an email labelled works update 29th March with an attachment of 14 photos!!

Preparing for the reinforced concrete reinforcement of basement over the pit and around the stone walls. Preparing for small underground water container and two other more underground containers for pump and other use.

Attaching 14 photos. Also I was thinking of using a web based photo share site to keep you updated. Let me know what you think.

M.

What did the photos show –well not just the house but other exciting details. In the first photo there was a view of the narrow street above our house with one of the builders loading bags either into or out of a small mechanised cart – but beyond him was a view of Maria's kefenion with Maria herself. She was standing in front of her establishment hopefully anticipating a busy day as she was holding a bowl of some greens (horta ? possibly) in front of her perhaps hoping to tempt the no doubt hungry builders to a lavish home cooked lunch.

Several years before we had seen our house we had walked up to the village and stopped with her for a drink to be confronted by a busy lunch time sitting of some three of four tables of customers all tucking into large hot meals. As we had only called by for drinks and mezes in the evening and were usually the only customers, in deed , she normally dashes in and brings out a table and chairs when you arrive giving the impression that she is also surprised to see customers . Well it is around a kilometre up a steep incline from the main village at sea level so we had been surprised by the extent of her clientele. On that occasion most of the diners were somewhat dusty and wore overalls and she later explained that they were builders renovating the house opposite her. Hopefully, she would gain some new custom from our builders.

Road Blocks

The small road was shown in another photo as blocked again, this time by a small lorry that was having bags of cement off-loaded onto the same barrow. Further pieces of the jigsaw puzzle that was the building work could be pieced together from the photos – the alley way to the house 'dog-legged' down past the other small houses –one had a new looking table and chair outside. My imagination worked overtime –was this a property rented out and was the building work going on whilst they stayed going to cause any friction in the future for us. More than likely it was a table put there by the owners to observe what was hap-pening over a glass or two of wine. The alley way swung to the right down a series of shallow steps but the photo revealed some temporary cement ramps that had been constructed to allow passage of the trol-ley up and down. Further close examination revealed the legs of a chair and a foot, no doubt of another onlooker –possibly the man I had given some of the almonds to that we had found when first clearing the house.

Well it all looked very organised as Manos had promised us all that time ago.

There were photos of stockpiles of cement bags, bags of what looked like grit, and other bags of waste earth. Also the photos appeared to show 4 different builders -all quite dusty of varying ages and all wear-ing hats and jumpers!

The most significant event was inside the house. One photo showed a fuse box on the wall inside the door whilst others showed that the massive hole for the cess-pit had been covered over –with what looked like a mesh and red earth. We assumed this was in advance of the concrete skim for the floor. More intriguingly some new pits had been created at the edge of the room. There had been some discussion about this back at the planning stage when mention was made of us-ing some under-floor space for the reserve cold water tank and for the pump and water heater. There was also debate about the possibility of some storage compartments as we were both conscious of the need for as much storage as was possible if living in this small space was to be as comfortable as possible. This conversation like so many others had not been forgotten and Manos was incorporating some under floor storage. Anyway, it was good to see the ground floor restored as the two and a half meter deep pit had always rather scared me – although the scariest part had been the cost of actually digging it. Still I tried to take some comfort in the earlier comments from Manos that the solid nature of the rock foundations would allow some reduction in subse-quent reinforcement work,(and costs)

Other photos taken the same week showed the street (just an alley-way really) in front of the house once more filled up with red soil and piles of rocks.

More reassuringly there was another picture showing the street clear again. Under the photo was the caption – "we promised to clean every day at end of works"

Manos was really into the idea of web storage of pictures for projects. Whilst we looked at ours he had also posted a series each for other current projects which included the restoration of an old stone wind-mill, another small stone house, a hillside outdoor spa, a shop with beautiful painted concrete display shelves a painted adobe style house and a spectacular hillside new build. The last was on the hill above our village and used vast quantities of cut stone both for the house and the garden and terraces walling. This may be an explanation for where the stones out our floor tank excavation had gone. Perhaps some of their materials had comeback the other way; certainly the scale of their house would allow it. There were rooms there much larger than our total house volume.

It was good to see the range of projects and it confirmed our faith in the capabilities of Manos – a faith that we had both shared from our very first discussions with him about what would be possible with a small and simple basic stone house.

The following weekend, at the end of the first week of April, the progress update started with a photo of the ground floor with the pit still covered over and a wire reinforcement mesh overlaying it. There were also several boxes of shuttering at the corners where the pump and cold-water reserve tank would be sited. More interestingly there was evidence of the source of the shuttering. At the back of the room was half of the large wooden box that we had found upstairs when were first clearing out the house. The one that we had speculated with Manos whether it had arrived seventy years ago in a flying boat. Whatever, it was now being recycled as part of the building process- very green!
A comment had been placed on the site under the last picture- "the electrician and the plumber are to come next. Pre-piping and or piping will be inserted"

So some real progress

Friday morning and an email alerted me to updated photos on the website. I checked our project set to find three new photos of the ground floor and as promised there appeared to have been some recent activity of a "pre-piping" nature. New white conduits for cables ran straight across the floor between the box shuttering, over the top of the metal reinforcing mesh and up the walls. More random blue hosing with shiny metal ends snaked out of the boxes and curled on the floor. It looked like someone had taken the water hoses of a dozen washing machines and scattered them around the house – I had to hope someone knew what they were doing. Again the photos showed signs of past activity none of the workforce appeared on camera.
The next day a new email alert appeared –so soon – good! We knew it was Greek Easter this week and I was realistic about a potential slow-down in progress but no – the new pictures showed more activity.
The first showed a cement mixer and the motorised cart complete with what I regarded as three quarters of the work-force i.e. three rather cement spattered guys. Mr tall and dark –the youngest, the other two

were shorter, fit looking and wearing the popular local builders protective headgear of baseball caps.

(I must get their names from Manos but this was so strange –whenever any building works are completed at home by the end of day one; along with detailed instructions for their particular beverage requirements you usually have heard complete family histories, ailment lists and hobbies and interests. Our last chimney sweep had provided all of this in a two hour period along with interesting anecdotes about other customers.   All wearing short sleeved T shirts in what appeared to be bright sunshine in the narrow alleyways outside the house. There were still a large pile of bags of building materials in the second photo but the third and fourth were evidence of more progress. We had a concrete floor !! The entire ground floor was filled with what looked like still wet concrete with blue hose ends emerging at intervals and little islands of wooden shuttered boxes.

Another week passed by. We had realised that the weekend seemed to be the time for Manos to take stock and send us an update with new photos of the progress that week.

The next set of photos were even more dramatic- arriving on the following Friday. They were notified as additions to the project web-site so they carried no commentary. The first one was dramatic and a little hard to comprehend. It showed the timbers of the ground floor ceiling –which economically doubled as the floorboards for the first floor room- with the old 'ladder style' staircase leaning against the wall but two things were markedly different. Firstly, the wall was no longer smoothly rendered and grey – it was rough stone and honey coloured. Secondly, day light streamed through the hatch opening to the first floor- the stones on one of the walls were almost bleached out in the suns rays – how was this?

The second photo provided more clues- it was taken from the street, looking up at the front of the house, and the blue sky could be seen clearly through the two windows upstairs –the roof was off !

Further photos confirmed this, particularly the two that showed all the roof tiles stacked neatly in the narrow street outside the front door, or more correctly, where the front door used to be. This was gone along

with the door frame and the window frames. A lot of progress had been made in the last week although ironically the house now fitted the modest description I had been using to people who had visions of Mediterranean terraces and infinity pools –"No, no – we have bought an old terraced house –just four stone walls "

and now that was what we were seeing in the photograph –very sobering, really.

The walls inside were also very different in appearance having been stripped of their rendering coating, which admittedly had been of variable condition. Downstairs it had been so dark that it had always been difficult to truly establish the condition of the walls. But now it was clear that there was some attractive stonework – it was this that Manos wanted to highlight where the much discussed niches were to be formed.

145

The use of the web-site for project updates had another advantage as Manos had added a number of other projects there which certainly reminded us of the range of his capabilities and helped reassured us that this project should not present him with any great technical difficulty
The next email also confirmed what was happening –
"Thanks for the sms - as you see we took away all internal plaster and transported away debris. Took away tiles and stocked the very good ones.
I try to act like the James Bond way (visit – act-clean-go away) so that I cause minimum disturbance to the village.
Next Steps:
Open niches
Reinforce

I saw Maria this morning in the town square –she looks great.
She was asking me when you were planning to come and if you were going to stay in Kritsa.
No, I am not on holiday. But it seems I will be needing one very soon...
Best regards

The next photographs that appeared on the web-site were unlabelled but appeared to show the "niche work" starting. There was some support bars downstairs holding the upstairs floor joists up and a pair of small trestles supporting some scaffolding planks. Atop this with his back to us –reassuringly wearing shorts, was one of the builders. Behind him the wall appeared different colours and some mortar pointing activity was taking place. The second picture showed a similar scene upstairs, minus the builder, we knew it was upstairs – the blue sky was showing through the roof rafters were the tiles had been removed. The final picture showed the street.
Again, this was progress but it was now four weeks from our return visit ! The statement by Manos when the date had been given some weeks earlier –" June, you will be staying in the house!!" looked like an act of bravado –we would see.

146

After a week without updates I rang the office to speak to Manos. No he wasn't there at the moment – Early evening Crete time might be better- or ring him on his mobile on site.

I did that –"Hello, how are you – yes progress is good but the niche work is very slow."

I reminded him of our imminent arrival- you are coming so soon, "yes, I thought –only a week after the completion date in the contract!"

The house will not be finished ? –No, No … you must stay in the Kritsa house – more comfortable"

Well yes, it had a roof for starters. We will be there for two weeks – there must be time to discuss completion details –"Of course, Yes that will be most useful"

The friends of ours who had been on the island on holiday at the same time we had first seen the house had emailed with some exciting news. They were seriously looking at a plot of land on the south of the island – they had even been told that a new house could be built in six months!

Which six months ? We would need to talk.

The end of May and we were back in Crete again. As soon as we ar-rived – it was the clear skies, the heat, the rather random traffic arrangements, the ability to wander into a restaurant after 11p.m. and be welcomed as customers – we were back!

The next day was a Saturday but we visited the house anyway and we were pleased with the progress. The new floor skim was down covering the drain excavations, the interior walls were stripped of their old plas-ter to reveal the honey coloured stonework. Work had begun on the niches but the ground floor ceiling –which doubled up as the floor to the room upstairs was still in place. The house seemed much lighter – then we remembered – the roof tiles were neatly stacked up in the street and the first floor was open to the sky. Still it was definitely progress. There was more evidence around with bags of waste render-ing neatly stacked – the tracked trailer for conveying materials up the steps and the little concrete ramps temporarily placed in the steps to ease it's progress. There also seemed quite a large delivery of bags of cement.

Friends of ours from Sussex were also staying in the area and were keen to see the works after so many months of being updated with progress or in some cases the lack of the same. We arranged to meet them and bring them up the hill from the town.

It was good to show the house and the renovations in progress to our friends although I could see them thinking that there was still a whole lot more to be done – something we couldn't deny.

We called Manos on his mobile and left a message that we had seen the progress and would like to meet up to discuss things. That evening there was a returned call from him–"Hi, everything is ok in the house for you? – where are you now" We were having supper in the village –"Good, I will call there and see you" A little while later the new company van arrived and we saw him, the office agent and his dog. It was great to meet again and hugs and handshakes with introductions to our friends who rightly considered ten o'clock a time to finish supper rather than begin it. We chatted over mezas and wine in the warm evening air in restaurant under a leafy tree – catching up on news and skirting around the fact that the contract had stipulated a May completion date. Eventually, there was an apology –" a lot of projects have had to be finalised at the same time, it has been very difficult, yours was late starting, some of the other projects were more stressfull….. the explanation hung in the warm mediterranean air …." Are you comfortable in the house?" It was difficult in this atmosphere and climate and good company to raise any anger –

Some matters of detail were raised – "the stone walls are good – I am thinking of more exposed stone and less plaster. The "gniting (a steel reinforcing mesh for earthquake protection is not necessary –the rock foundations and chain reinforcement will be sufficient. We must consider the niches- on site – and the terrace will still be in wood and pressed concrete on top of the metalwork. We still need to get light into the house –we can look at this tomorrow.

Let's meet up at the house first thing tomorrow and look at the works." Conversation turned to less sensitive matters and eventually we ambled downhill to our temporary holiday home.

The next day we were up bright and early to meet up at the house but just before we left a text arrived – a problem with stones – but not at the house –troublesome kidney stones for Manos – meeting postponed until tomorrow!

Still we were up and about early so we set of to the east of the island to get to Sitia in time to look round the shops. The verges were full of flowering shrubs and the roads quiet making for a pleasant drive for the hour or so that the it took us. The shops were good – mostly small individual and usually run by the owner as is the usual pattern on the island, assuring the customer of individual attention. We found coloured designer kitchen accessories in bright oranges, reds and lime green, stylish enough to be left on display. A catalogue was taken for future reference as such items seemed premature for the roofless four walls. Another shop was a small supermarket styled builders merchants with some useful appliances for when we arrived at the stage of thinking of appliances! A leisurely lunch at a restaurant next to the harbour and a swim on the way back home rounded off the outing. The house would have to wait until tomorrow.

The next morning found us full of optimism driving up the hill to the house. The sun was bright, the air already warm, there were even birds singing as we walked down the village's alleyways to the house. Today, true to his word Manos was present; as were a small team of builders. There had been some progress the previous day. The floor had been removed and there were more large holes in the walls (or niches, as Manos more fondly describe them.) The effect looked to us, in any event, to be less planned and more the result of some explosive events inside the house which had removed the floor and blown large cavities in the inside walls.
Manos did his best to allay our fears.
"The floor boards are stacked outside – I am negotiating to use a storage room opposite to avoid removing materials we will be re-using."
We were introduced to the three builders –one Greek with two Albanian assistants. It looked like hot and dusty work in a confined space but everyone seemed happy enough and Manos described the progress

to date positively and outlined the next stages of work to us. We adjourned to Maria's kafenion for welcome drinks and we were set a task. "You need to look around at the patterns of the traditional doors, windows and shutters to make a choice for your house. Anything can be made but you must decide on patterns and colour." For a house that appeared to be disappearing the more we saw it this did feel like a step in the right direction.

"We can meet again here tomorrow with ideas and at that time discuss room heights." OK, that seemed like a plan, tomorrow it would be – we needed to look at doors and windows!

The Doors

This task could have been accomplished at home in Sussex as we had over the years amassed quite a collection of pictures of doors, shutters and windows taken in a number of Cretan towns and villages. These had been acquired a number of years before we had a personal interest or even investment in our own set of doors and windows on the island. Now, with only twenty-four hours notice we had the opportunity to apply all this redundant knowledge of Cretan architectural details to selecting our own. It seemed quite a responsibility. We had already arranged to meet some friends for dinner near the harbour so we resisted the temptation to drive further afield to the towns further east or on the south coast. Instead, over a cold drink in the village kafenion we talked about our ideas for doors, windows and shutters. There was also the opportunity of looking around our own village to compare styles. I also remembered that some four years of photos were stored on my ipod so that was another option to help with our choice. In the end, after a stroll around both the resort town and our hill village we concluded that the simpler the pattern was for them, the better. We had seen a number of shutters and doors that echoed the simple pattern used at home in Sussex as what we thought of as farmhouse style, plain tongue and groove boards. "Room heights"– not something I had any experience of choosing for a house.

When we met at the house the next morning the our ideas for a simple pattern were met with cheerful approval by Manos as was some traditional hinge shapes for the shutters which we had seen and photographed in a nearby village. We again adjourned to the safety and quiet of the nearby kefenion as the builders were continuing with their demolition programme. This time it involved standing atop the walls and bashing away at the same walls with sledge hammers –the wall and loose fill material that apparently was binding the stones together dropped heavily and all too easily to the ground, two floors below. It was explained this was to get a level around the top of the walls to install the "chains." This term had led to some misunderstanding- it appeared it was derived from a french origin and was a generic term for reinforcement. What would happen was that the builders would fabricate reinforced concrete beams on site using metal rods that they were bending and linking together on a hand jig "in the street" ; these would be placed in wooden shuttering at the top of the walls. Concrete

would then be mixed up and poured into these moulds making bespoke re-inforced concrete beams on top of the walls. Simple and effective, I was just glad that it wasn't me that was carrying the buckets of wet concrete up two storeys in thirty degrees of heat to make them. During one of our morning walks around the village we were attracted to loud noises coming from a narrow street at the top of the village. The noise became louder as we approached it's source until at an open it was deafening and we realised from the clouds of dust emerging and the snaking feed line from a compressor parked out of sight around a corner that we were witnessing and experiencing drain excavations. It may well have been the same folk that had

constructed the hole for our tank – we were amazed that people in the village were still talking to us , and maybe more amazing that they could still hear any of our replies!

By our next site visit the beams appeared to have been finished although the shuttering was still in place but downstairs the piles of rubble and dust had been carefully sorted into piles of reusable stones and dozens of bags of the smaller rubble and earth. As a building site it was certainly tidy but I think the space constraints meant that this was the only practical way to work – even so, it still impressed us. Standing on next door's terrace looking across the top of the house we were able to remind ourselves that this position and the view was what had first attracted us to the house. It still took our breath away, looking across the roofs of the village houses, out over the olive groves and down to the harbour and the deep turquoise sea. Beyond that the causeway to the island and the distant hazy mountains completed the view – it was truly spectacular.

Our revery was interrupted by the arrival of Manos – morning's greetings were exchanged. "I have an important question for you" he said, ominously. "The outside – the stonework; how do you want it – rendered, bare stonework?"

We thought bare stonework .

Of course it wasn't that simple – it never was! If it was to be bare stonework, Manos patiently explained, we would need to decide the colour of the pointing between the stones. We were getting more used to this process and the multiple choice options.

We all agreed that the concept of the whole project was, as far as possible, to preserve the look of the house. So was it possible for the pointing and stonework cleaning to have an end objective of looking as near as possible to how the house walls looked at the moment. This was met with approval –"Of course- I think the walls have had some slight red staining from the red earth in the "loose fill" between the stones – we can match the pointing back to that"

Another decision on the project – we all adjourned to the cafenion for refreshments. This was always an opportunity to discuss progress and to attempt to get a vague idea of the sequence of work that was planned and also an indication of timescales – although the concept of timings was accepted by us to have some "inbuilt elasticity" all deadlines were now viewed as no more than 'aspirational.'

We also felt in need of some reassurance that the building site would become a house and an explanation of the stages between that end objective and the current state of the house might provide us with a little of this.

Over our coffee refills the next actions were outlined by Manos.

"Once the concrete beams are finished the stonework will be rebuilt around them. The stonemasons can create any additional niches inside, while they are here. They will also create the two new windows and make good afterwards.

The next big task is to create the metal structure and this will support the roof the new balcony, the new spiral stairs to the balcony and the staircase between the two floors.

I have a metalworker in town who is coming next week to give a price for this work but I am confident that he will be able to do this."

There was further discussion about the proposed metal-work; it would make it easier to install the glass floor panels that were planned to bring light down into the ground floor.

Once the metal was installed the stairs fixed to them would give access for more building work – the new sun terrace floor, the new roof. There was still plenty of stonework – once the new windows were created then all the stonework would be cleaned, inside and outside, before the re-pointing could be started.

The re-pointing would only be done after the electrical wiring and the first fix plumbing had been completed

The first photos that were posted on the web-site were rather alarming. The front wall looked like someone had driven a car at it or a high velocity shell had provided a direct hit- it must be the preparations for the new ground floor window – but it looked awful, a large irregular hole, embellished by a pile of rubble on the floor below it! We kept our patience and a week later we were rewarded by a couple of photos of the new window and the stone masonry around it all made good and matching the original wall- phew, we were relieved. The window was framed at the top by a reclaimed timber of old wood to match the other window frames –it looked great. Through the new window frame we could see the roof tiles still piled up in the alleyway outside. There was still a lot of work to be done!

Heavy Metal

Further updates followed within days; the first showing new niches that had been created in the wall in the area earmarked for the kitchen. It looked like the stonemasons were still in town.

Then, in the first week in July a dramatic addition; tall black metal girders rose above the top wall of the house, one in each corner framing the building. This must be the start of the metal work reinforcement that Manos had described during our visit in May.

It would have the dual purpose of supporting the two staircases as well as providing the necessary earthquake protection without the need to underpin the stone walls. The cynic in me alarmingly imagined the house after an earthquake where we would perhaps be sitting upstairs on our metalwork frame ; no doubt shaken and stirred, whilst below us was a pile of rubble that used to be our house.

Over the next two weeks further instalments of posted photos showed the gradual creation of a very solid looking metal lattice work that created the beams for the first floor, supports for the stairs from the ground floor

The whole thing was a box girder-like construction in black metal and looked very industrial and contrasted strongly with the natural and irregular stonework of the walls. What were we doing to this poor old traditional stone house ? As the days went on successive photos showed additions to the constructionWe could only imagine what the village residents were making of this metal creation going on in their midst – we knew the village had the normal level of interest in anything new that was happening – this must be fueling speculation. The industrial work was more like a commercial building. What sort of speculation were we starting ? The first mini fitness centre in the village – a micro branch of the local supermarket

The shape of the top terrace could now be seen; with the bonus that photos showing this picked up the views from the top of the house with the beautiful views over the village roofs to the bay as well as the mountains. Individual photos showed the core for the spiral staircase to the terrace, a single metal pole that bisected the house from ground level up to some two meters above the roof-line (or more correctly, where he roof-line would be when there was a roof. The works were starting to "flesh out" what for some months now had looked like a large stone box. Several of the later photos finally put a face to the creator of this metallic masterpiece. Standing atop the lattice frame

work of the new terrace was a dark bearded stranger, wearing lilac shorts and a T shirt and proudly holding his welding tongs. His safety gear seemed to comprise a headband, short socks and glasses (untinted). Hopefully, the welding mask or goggles were out of camera shot! In the later pictures the cross-pieces on the terrace had been filled in with a network of wires, as thick as fingers, to provide the support for the terrace which we had been told would be pressed concrete over a layer of insulation.

The end of July brought the first pictures of the stairs. The staircase from the ground floor was a straight flight up half of the back wall of the house, turning through ninety degrees to come back along the right hand side wall, towards the front door. The stairs themselves were only a metal framework and we had earlier discussed them with Manos at the planning stage. We has seen them as being an almost organic shape perhaps framed in plaster with stone or tiled treads. This shape seemed too linear –we would need to talk- but at least we had stairs again !

In the middle of this flurry of activity at the house , the evidence of which we were seeing in the photos, another mysterious note arrived from Manos.

House thoughts

Hi there,

Sorry but it has been and is very hectic in order to be able to have a serene conversation.....I am also thinking of the staircase (and not only...)**, the bean or whatever shape, the encumbrance or not of the 4 steps in the livable house as well as the age going on and the necessity to get up to the mezzanine in a comfy way...especially if one has to face the spiral steps up to the terrace and the view....I am thinking....I think I will spend some time up in your house tomorrow to go on thinking...Sure I have the ideas...please do not hesitate to write to me your thoughts and ideas....I would like to have these written down... even if just scattered thoughts.... I would like to read them ...not to speak right now....

** I am thinking of how nice the stone is against this metallic structure.....hesitating in plastering it....thinking ...could use the vertical beams and metallic elements to create hidden illumination and in a way expand-illusionary-the dimensions of the house...thinking...please I would love to have your thinking......

M.

- we like the bare stone and could resist plastering
- the Egg/Bean will be smooth and contrasts
- we like metal elements –you talked earlier about "weathering" and fixing corrosion – would this look purple/black/orange iridescent-like ? that would be good particularly with the stone.

157

- Hidden illumination sounds good – we wondered about commercial/shop fitting spot lights downstairs –clamped to beams - moveable–we have seen curly cable wiring linked to this – (HI-Tech book 1980)-could be different colours.
- "Expanding illusionary" – maybe the glass plate in ground floor ceiling should be central in the room–as a larger block –linking the spaces –that way natural light could transfer down – at night artificial light could transfer up giving a more subdued light interest upstairs and expanding the space. May also be more functional for placing furniture upstairs.

Overall, the house is traditional outside , not very noticeable, almost secret in the village –friends from England couldn't find it – one needed talking in over a mobile! –even local friends did not know it was there despite growing up in the village.

Then you open the door and inside should be a surprise! The mix of metal and stone – light coming down through the building – and the unusual Bean/Egg bathroom pod.

A larger glass plate surface in ceiling would open up the house.

If we don't have plastering we could use old shutters and wood on parts of the stone walls –like in Kritsa – perhaps supported from the iron frame by wires/chains to fix things to/ break up the stone –but could be moved/resited.

Egg/Bean - smooth contrasting with the stone walls.

Organic shape, soft , the stairs curving behind cocooned in the egg and through rather than sitting on top – not visible as they climb the egg.

If they curved around to face the front door it would create more space for the seating area at the back left hand side.

It would be interesting to see a Cad drawing of this (if it would not send Dimitri crazy?)

The inside could be coloured- the brighter/lighter the better.

Prefer white on outside.

You had an idea a while ago for "punching holes" in one wall for shafts of light.

Could we use this in the egg – light in and out – we thought of prisms – dismantle old chandeliers from ebay.

158

Some lights on top of egg could light the stairs, organic , sunk-in.
We could add a shower head with LEDS –(available on ebay!-red or blue) so when in shower you have lit water and light from outside like stars.
Door could be like a space ship hatch.

Stairs

If the stairs were to start at floor level , facing the front door –the first turn could be a triangular stair –like in Kritsa – not a square half landing –then the stairs would wrap around and go through the Egg in a more coherent way and lead more naturally from an open floor area rather than taking wall space.

Floor – the white stones we chose would give light- perhaps they could also be incorporated into the stair treads. We will send a scanned picture where a floor has used some broken tiles as a mosaic to break up the regularity –this might be good to outline the less regular egg shape. Perhaps incorporating a few, random shiny ceramics –sparingly but in a similar light shade.

These are our first thoughts –we will scan and email any useful pictures/sketches..

The next set of photos were a bit more mysterious: an email told me there was a new picture; it was hard to make out at first but he caption explained –"wrong steps delivered…." It showed a collection of metal steps on the floor and a pair of legs and arms- ending in what looked like industrial gloves – forget the steps –safety wear had been delivered ! The error was obvious –the plan was to form the steps for the spiral stairs to the roof terrace from steel mesh, this would allow light down the stair well- these would not !

Oh well, still progress of a sort.

The construction of the terrace framework also allowed Manos to post a series of photos of the view; and it was spectacular, better than we imagined. The photos were taken looking out from the terrace, starting with a view back into the village over the roofs towards our local, Maria's kafenion with the road to the little church and village graveyard snaking up and around the hill at the back of the houses. In front of the house the olive groves stretched down to the coast with glimpses of the road up to the village. On the left we could see one of the near-by hamlets on a patch of high ground before the deep turquoise of the sea and the hills that formed the lagoon across the bay. Straight ahead was a view of distant mountains with the town much nearer in the foreground with the harbour and bay in front of it and beyond that the causeway that took the road to the other side of the lagoon. This was the natural airport used some seventy years ago by the Imperial Airways flying boats that broke their journey to India and beyond with overnight stops in the lagoon. To the right there were more views over our neighbours roofs and gardens, complete with chickens and goats; the local mountains stretched away up to the right, towering into the sky. We knew the views would be good but what we were seeing in the pictures exceeded our expectations.

The next update was different. On the last visit we had chosen the pattern for the door, windows and shutters; now we were seeing the fruits of those decisions. The set of pictures were taken in a carpenter's workshop with the windows and shutters neatly stacked up in clean, new wood. We knew these contrasted with the original, paint distressed and aged windows that had been in the house but those were really beyond repair. We still hoped to salvage some of the wood for decorative use in the house and we loved their weather worn paint finish. The following day the next set of pictures showed some new scenes of mayhem in the house. It was called "niche work" but looked like vandalism. Below the new staircase the stonemasons had burrowed into the wall and a large cavity some two by one metre square had been created. A similar attack had taken place on the inside of the front wall, unfortunately this had been created below the newly created window with it's carefully created new stonework. We could only assume that people knew what they were doing to our little house, on our behalf almost two thousand miles away.

A further update later the same week carried details of dramatic progress on the exterior. The external walls had been pressure washed to clean the stones and remove the old pointing from between the stonework. It was our first view of the new small window for the bathroom and it was pleasing to see the way this lined up with the original doorway and the new large window in the front wall. We were starting to get a better idea of the external view of the house when finished.

Around the same time I booked flights for a viewing visit. Summer in Sussex had been so wet and miserable we couldn't wait until September, our normal time for visits. We would go in August and tolerate or revel in the heat. Recent progress on the house had been good but the whole project had been like that with progress in fits and starts. We knew that there were a number of factors against progress: access was difficult, vans and lorries had to be left two streets away; the house was small making work sequential rather than consecutive; inevitably it commanded less of Manos's attentions as a project manager compared with larger more expensive projects.

By providing the date of our next unplanned visit we hoped that progress would be accelerated. This seemed to be the case.

In early August, on a day out in Rye, Sussex I checked my emails over coffee to see that there were some more photo posts. They were exciting –the metal mesh treads of the spiral stairs were laid out on the ground, like wedges of a cake and they were the right ones this time. The other photos were close ups of the treads – so we could see they were the mesh ones to let light through – they also showed the construction and although they looked fine there was definitely a hand crafted look about them. We guessed that they were made locally by hand and later photos showed them being carefully welded into place on the metal column to provide the spiral staircase to the terrace. It looked great, almost sculptural – like a set of dragonfly wings overlapping each other silhouetted against the sky. Another milestone in progress.

Two weeks before our planned visit a set of pictures were posted showing the roof joists –we had agreed earlier that we would reuse any sound wood and the sturdy, unplaned, rounded, original roof timbers were good candidates for this. The pictures showed them re-installed at the top of the house – trimmed to accommodate the roof terrace at the back and awaiting the reproofing which would also see the recycling of the old clay tiles.

The August visit

For the first visit to the house on this trip we fortified ourselves with a breakfast in town near the harbour; the cold frappe coffees and hot crepes would set us up for the visit. There had been a gap of over a week since the last set of photos had been posted on the web-site so we weren't sure what progress to expect. The last photos had shown the roof timbers in place – there had been discussion about these – they were the original roof joists and we had agreed to re-use them if this was possible. We hoped that the absence of photos was not because there wasn't any progress to show but that Manos wanted to surprise us with whatever had been completed.

We parked the hire car off the road behind the church and walked through what we could start to describe as our village. We walked down the two sets of steps and past both kefenions into our "street" or, in truth, alleyway. Brilliant !!! we could see from the top of our alleyway that the roof, bare at the end of our last visit in June, had returned to it's rightful colour with a covering of red clay tiles. On reaching the house we discovered Iannis, the roof man gathering up the broken and surplus tiles; (for the roof we had tried to follow our

policy of re-using whatever was possible in the house - to go some way towards offsetting the injection of concrete, steel and glass into the project.) We also wanted the house to look as true to it's origins as possible from the outside. The restored roof was literally the "icing on the cake" –once we squeezed past the scaffolding the interior was amazing. When we last saw the "work in progress" back in mid-june it resembled a "stone tank" with stone reinforcement work being carried out, rather precariously atop the walls.

Since that time we had been updated over the internet with the building of the steelworks frame for the first floor and the terrace; the installation of the staircase, the spiral stairs to the and the creation of two windows as well as several niches! The interior was still very much a "work-in-progress building site" but it was very reassuring for us to see the progress first hand. Movement through the house was precarious to say the least. There were still some blocks of stone on the floor inside, planks and bags of cement. The holes in the floor were only half covered with planks and some surplus scaffolding was leaning against the wall. To get upstairs meant negotiating these random barriers and then using a metal stair frame with no step treads. Once up-stairs there were only two scaffolding planks laid across the metal framework as the floor. Using these I was able to negotiate my way onto the small spiral stairs up to the roof terrace. The terrace itself comprised more of the metal framework with a lattice work of iron rods criss-crossing it. This allowed a clear view through the two storeys to the floor of the house some distance below.

It was certainly uncomfortable but the compensation was that it al-lowed me at last to see the view from what would become our terrace.

Despite the awkward access the view was spectacular! The house seemed in the centre of the village but at the same time because the ground dropped away, it seemed on the edge – with clear views to the sea and across the village to the mountains. There were also interest-ing views back into the village with glimpses of the road to Maria's, the road around the hillside to the small church there as well as the road up from town. The view was every bit as good as we had hoped when the terrace had been planned. It was the view that we had talked to Manos about – it seemed so long ago – hell it was long ago – but the wait was paying off ! Across the olive groves that lay between the village and the town we could glimpse the buildings at the coast. The sea shimmered beyond them before the familiar contours of the other side of the lagoon. As a bonus there was the view in the distance of the mountains, a faint shade of pinky grey, that lay between us and the other side of the island. "You have to come and see this view..." I called - and after an awkward climb up, S agreed that the view made all our efforts to date more than worth it.

There were other pleasant surprises- the stonework was much more interesting and varied in colour that it looked in photos. The new window downstairs opened the space up and the metalwork reinforcement had a solid sculptural quality and we agreed with Manos that a feature could be made of this rather than employing some clumsy attempts to disguise or hide this.

One of the best features was the look of the spiral staircase – from below the metal mesh treads resemble insect wings and had a particular beauty that we had not anticipated.

Iannis explained that the "architectonis" had already been and we had missed him – no matter we had seen the progress and we were happy again.

We spent the rest of the day catching up with friends in town and in the village we were staying in.

This included a walnut and raki reunion with the lovely old couple next door to the village house we were borrowing.

On our next visit to the house allowed us to take in the changes at a better pace and absorb what the house was becoming as the ideas formed over conversations and doodles, as well as proper drawing, were beginning to take shape in space, stone and steel. The reality was not so easy to comprehend as we were currently viewing the house in an x-ray vision way –without windows, floors and stair treads- providing a view from the ground floor of the blue sky through what would become the first floor and the roof terrace.

We desperately latched onto any element of the building works that provided a view of a finished element or surface but these were few. The top ceiling had been created under the clay tile roof and this comprised new light coloured planks laid over the old dark beams. But close examination of these was made precarious as the first floor room lacked a floor and any scrutiny of the ceiling was made from the lattice work of steel beams –with the drop through to the ground- I thought of the scary classic photos of the New York steeplejacks lunching whilst sitting astride girders hundreds of feet up in the air and told myself to stop being such a wimp. Still it gave the taking of any photos to mark progress an added element of drama as you had to remember not to step two foot to the right, and ten foot down, whilst composing a shot!

One morning, after one of our regular progress meeting with Manos and builders we were walking past the main village church when we bumped into one of the ladies that we had met earlier and had on that occasion given us a huge slab of the cinnamon flavoured church bread, called artos. Today, in the bright morning sunshine she was lugging a large shopping bag whilst negotiating some uneven steps down into the village from the church. She was again dressed in black and her head was covered with a black scarf. I guessed she was coming from the church. We said good morning and offered to help her and her bag down the steps. Initially, our offers were greeted with a warm smile

167

but a refusal to give up her heavy bag. I don't think we worried her as she seemed to recognise us but, sadly, I couldn't hep thinking the effect that a similar situation would have in England on an elderly lady alone in a village churchyard. We compromised, I carried her bag, S took her arm then as the three of us negotiated the steps the small lady showed greater than anticipated agility by thrusting her arm into the shopping bag I was now carrying to produce a great chunk of the church bread. We narrowly avoided all of us breaking our ankles but seconds later we were at her front door which turned out to be opposite the second kefenion in the main street and just at the top of the steps down to our house. The lady introduced herself as Maria , no surprise there and we said our good byes.

The story continued the next day when our early morning visit to the house/ building site to meet Manos found him above our house talking to Maria who became very animated when she saw us and after polite hellos had some 90 mph conversation with Manos which provoked him to laughter. "She wants to buy you drinks in the kefenion –she says you are her lovely new neighbours, I think you have been undertaking a new charm offensive in the village –with luck they will forget about all the earlier building noise and dust –and the grief they have been giving me about the small ramps down the steps!! Anyway, I have explained that we have a few minutes discussion at the house – she will watch for your return up the steps for the promised drink."

We said our goodbyes and went down to the house.

The new idea for today was the development of an earlier theme by Manos. "We should perhaps think of the house more as one space rather than two rooms" – this was not so difficult as apart from the metal structure and a couple of scaffolding boards there wasn't anything between the two floors. You stood downstairs where we were still trying to imagine the kitchen and look up through the first floor room with the spiral stairs, clean through to the mesh of the top terrace and on to the blue sky!

His idea was that along with the glass plate in the centre of the floor, designed to bring light to downstairs, we should also avoid closing off the floor between the two storeys. Lighting onto the stone walls would be used to emphasise the gaps at the side. This would give the impression of the floor "floating" between the two rooms. Certainly it would be an interesting and intriguing feature with light coming down at the side as well as through the centre panels.

The only downside seemed that there would be a whole new potential for losing things – something I was not actively looking for as – at the risk of repeating myself ,I already seemed to spend too much of my life "looking for things"! On balance , we decided it would be worth the risk and like so many decisions in this project discussed it, thought about it and arrived at a decision well in advance of anything likely to happen about the particular decision. Although, we had often discovered that Manos's questions and decisions had a logic to them in respect of their timing.

We were the "victims" of a friendly ambush when we went back up the steps – Maria lay in wait at her front door and insisted in steering both of us to the nearby kefenion where our "original Maria" was pleased to put out three chairs around the little blue metal table she had been sitting us and supply us all with limonadas at the expense and insistence of the new Maria.
We chatted in broken Greek and English; conversation being mostly confined to agreements about the beauty of the village, the view, the weather and our little house. After returning to her house once to collect some family photos to show us; I was steered by Maria "2" on another trip to her house but this time I was directed to our house with instructions to "go up to the top" from which I could see Maria who had emerged onto her balcony which was above us but only some fifty yards away!

On another day the phone rang at home, it was Manos. "Hi, I need to ask you something – outside, on the front wall of the house, do you want an outside light and if so, where ?"
The narrow alleyway down to the little house had a street light at the top end of it but a light on the house would be good. We asked for a couple of lights at the top of the front wall, just under the eaves which would allow light to wash down the front wall and highlight the stones. "Yes, of course, that was possible at this stage, before the stones had been pointed, good idea!"
A similar request had arrived shortly afterwards – "do you want a doorbell?" The favoured method of greeting we noticed in the village was for people to call from the street towards an open window – even when doorbells and knockers were in evidence. We decided that initial-

ly a doorbell might give a better clue that such greetings were specifically for us –so we said yes to a bell. We had realised quite some time earlier that such requests gave us a false sense of imminent completion and while I like to think that this was further proof of the architect's methodical and detailed approach to the project there had been some occasions when they felt like a diversionary tactic.

Much Later

The photo sharing site alerted me to new postings again. This time there were three: a close up of the outside stonework with the caption –pressure washing external walls before pointing. The second showed the guy doing the work – balanced on the scaffolding against the sea facing front wall. The final picture was of the hidden back wall of the house which was being plastered. Despite gloomy weather warnings for the eastern Med on the weekend weather maps in the UK papers, the sky was bright blue and clear –again! These pictures were followed two days later by the follow up pointing - again the sky was clear and blue and the walls really started to look finished with the new mortar against the cleaned stone walls.

Later that week the next photo update showed the start of the stonework re-pointing –the filling of the gaps between the stones with light coloured mortar made the walls much lighter. If this effect was the same on the bare inside walls then our fears about them being light enough may not be realised.

There was also evidence in the photos of a discussion we had had on the previous visit – we had felt a slight feeling of vertigo on the top terrace – this was over and above the drop seen through the whole building where the metalwork wasn't yet filled. The parapet wall itself just felt too low for safety so we suggested raising it. Manos welcomed this and said it would be an opportunity to make a ledge on the terrace for seating/ shelving. He had kept back some spare stones in the alleyway to use for this. The photos that were posted showed the terrace wall being raised , only by about a foot but this would be enough. The pictures that showed a cloudy sky; we had talked with Manos about the need to get the house weather tight before the autumn rains, was there enough time ?

The real breakthrough came with the next set of photos the following weekend. For the first time since the late spring that there was no scaffolding around the house ! This was quite a milestone - moreover the stonework had been pointed ... and it looked wonderful. It reminded us of what we had seen in the house on the day of the first viewing. It sat proudly and squarely at the end of the little alleyway – looking out down towards the bay. The front face of the house had a pleasing symmetry with the new ground floor windows matching up with the

171

original front doorway and windows. The stones had been highlighted by the new pointing and seemed to gleam in the bright sunlight; the overall impression was one of a new start for the little house – more of a makeover than a transformation –the original character and proportions that we had fallen in love with still shone through. The house exterior had been preserved and the intrusions of the new windows and revised roof had been accomplished with respect to the original house – this was important to us and we were pleased that all the discussions with Manos about options and possibilities had culminated in what we were now looking at on the mac screen. Yes, it was worth it and we knew it would look even better in real life.

Access to the new roof terrace had always been a matter for discussion. There would need to be a trade off between taking space from the small terrace and allowing an easy access. The planning consent for the terrace had been a difficult acquisition so any arrangements also had to be pretty unobtrusive. Fortunately, Manos had a cunning plan. It was a typical drawing from Manos, similar in style to others we had seen, hand-drawn like a little work of art with some colouring and notes in English and Greek . The email showed a rather a complex looking hatch which was made up of four panes of glass in a frame with a slot between two of them to accommodate a new strut to be fitted to the spiral stairs as a stay. This seemed to me to be a good idea as there was a slight movement at the top of the staircase , not surprising as supporting building work was not yet complete.

Progress seemed less dramatic for a couple of months, certainly compared to the flurry of activity through the summer and early autumn. We consoled ourselves that once the direct flights to the island ended for the winter we were unlikely to return until the spring. It was possible travel to the island through connections in Athens and we may well make use of this in the future – once the house was complete! We received a couple of update photos from Manos. These included the piping for an air conditioning unit which was chased into the stonework and a drain from the new terrace.
The next significant update did not arrive until the start of December. The first were a set of photos showing our doors, windows and shutters all stacked up in a workshop but painted in the blue/grey colour we had chosen with Manos during the last visit. It was good to see

these but I was becoming ever more anxious about the house being made weather-tight. Back in September Manos had agreed that the house needed to be secured against the elements before the winter rains arrived. We had experienced the intensity of these one late October on the island when roads looked like they were being washed away. The month saw a dialogue between us with me asking when the house would be sealed and him offering me reassurances that it was still sunny and dry on the island and for me not to worry for it would be done soon! One of the problems was getting the elusive electrician back on site to locate wiring for ceiling spots in the terrace floor before the floor was constructed. The delay was compounded when on the first visit the wiring was laid over the top of the metal framework rather than through it needing a second visit to reroute this.

In the event the concrete was place on the terrace two days before Christmas and Manos had the gall to tell me that it started raining as soon as they had finished !

Several weeks before this Manos had sent us one of his "Some Thoughts" emails, this time the subject was the bathroom. There were three pages of "thought" in notes and little sketched drawings.

The bathroom was always going to be an area that was affected by the size of the house. Under the stairs was the logical place to put it and we had agreed that from quite an early date. Some construction had taken place for it already, the creation of a new small window in the front wall, pipes for drainage and plumbing and the location of a cistern in a new wall niche. The issue that hadn't been finalised was the shape and construction materials to use for the bathroom along with the position of the door. Earlier plans ranged from the mildly eccentric "Egg" design for a wet-room with stairs cut into the roof of it to a simple straight wall constructed under the stairs. We had already chosen the bathroom fittings on an earlier visit when we had undertaken a number of visits to bathroom showrooms. These had been a revelation both in terms of the range of fittings available as well as the scale of the showrooms themselves, some of them were huge and I had already concluded the Greeks appeared ahead of us in terms of bathroom sophistication.

Thoughts

The ideas in the latest "Thoughts" email were a middle ground between the two extremes. The first page was a floor plan putting onto paper the various components we had discussed for the bathroom. It would occupy the whole length of the side wall of the house – to your right as you entered the house. But space would be compromised by the headroom under the stairs as the rose up the same wall. The lower space would contain a washing machine with the bathroom fittings in the area where there would be headroom, the sink, wc and shower would have to be crammed into the remaining space. To create a little more space Manos proposed curving the wall out into the room towards the foot of the stairs which started on the back wall before they 'dog-legged' through ninety degrees to continue up the back wall.

This curve out would be cut into next to the stairs to house a fridge freezer. The door into the bathroom was marked as being 1 metre wide and reaching to the ceiling, in the notes to the drawing he had drawn a sketch of the door with a description of "glass sandwich, transparent + glass internally to the 2 slates of glass with ping pong white balls (you are free for any other filling.)

There was also a description of the "internal belly expansion of the bathroom" sic, "this could be left empty or shelves could be created in: plexiglass, (milky) with or without internal lighting, wood, metal slate, gypsum panel, "many other thoughts......

So, certainly some thoughts to react to .....ping pong balls –I don't

think so! As with most of the ideas from Manos they were mostly good and broadly met our needs. Our reply tempered some of the 'creativity" of the plan – we felt the door was too big and the filling of balls or whatever might only draw attention to what was after all only the door to the bathroom – we suggested a smaller door in a pattern to match the front door. The "internal belly" idea was a good one, a smaller door would allow it to be larger and would help with space inside as well as creating a logical space for the fridge; this could perhaps be faced with a door made from recycled old wood from the house disguising the fridge/freezer and creating a cupboard space above.. As far as construction we wanted something solid and suggested a curved brick wall, plastered smooth to contrast with the stone walls.

The use of glass must be translucent but suggested restricting it to the back of some of the stair treads as had been previously suggested by Manos. We also added that the priority now is practicality and completion. We turned around the reply the next day in the hope that firming up on the details of the bathroom would speed progress. In the event apart from the return of the electrician and the concreting of the terrace nothing else happened prior to Christmas.

The holiday and New Year came and went and nothing was heard from the architect; my patience ran out mid-month and I enquired about progress. I received an apology from Manos with the information that the new brick wall for the bathroom would be constructed the following week.

Towards the end of the month a clutch of photo updates were posted; the first showing the start of the bathroom wall. This was followed by a set of pictures the following day showing that the wall had been completed, with a curve made out of the Mediterranean style 6 holed bricks laid on their end. The wall continued to the front door and a normal sized door opening had been made into the bathroom. The cupboard for the fridge/freezer had also been constructed –hooray! The new curved wall looked interesting in a photo taken from the front door and had the advantage of screening the stairs. There had also been some further work on the terrace with bricks being put in place around the new long lateral window to let light into upstairs from the terrace.

Around this time I discovered that I shared the same social networking site with Manos and by linking as friends I was able to see when he was on-line and therefore available for questioning. This proved to be useful in getting clarification on what work was scheduled and when – at least all the time some kind of schedule was being worked to!

The start of February saw the first pictures of the interior stone walls after cleaning and re-pointing. In earlier discussions we had weighed up the merits of bare stonework against re-plastering. We had agreed with Manos that it was worth seeing what the bare stones looked like when they were cleaned and re-pointed. If we were unhappy with the finish there was still the option of plastering. My main reservation had been whether it would make the house too dark but Manos had suggested that by using a light colour for the pointing that would be less likely. It certainly looked as if we had made the right decision; the stones looked wonderful. The first pictures showed the terrace and upstairs with the metal spiral staircase contrasting with the cleaned stonework. The floorboards had not yet been laid upstairs making the operation more difficult with the stonemason presumably balancing on the steelwork and scaffolding planks. Progress was going on apace; the next day another three photos were posted showing the stonewalls on the ground floor. Often it took a few viewings of the new photos to pick up all the interesting details – it was certainly remote renovation but we had entrusted Manos with the project management of the works and we were happy with the results to date.

Often it was when we were in conversation with people back in England that we felt defensive. There was often questioning about the way the project was evolving, not been built to a hundred percent fixed design, the wisdom of trusting a "foreigner", the gloomy recounting of stories of others who had been "ripped off" and of course why was it taking so long? I felt that all of these criticisms could be defended against, with the exception of the last.

The evolutionary nature of the project was a good thing and we had no problem with that. I am confident with my own judgement on people to trust. I am also not keen in listening to other people's sad tales of disasters.

The time delay was something we were managing. We had always seen it as a long-term project and we were enjoying the process Also we found it hard to remain angry with Manos for very long and his kind offer of accommodation in the already renovated house had helped with our own ideas as well as allowing us to experience living in another village where we had made some new friends. It always seemed less of a problem when we were on the island –maybe it was

just a mindset; certainly the island had a very ancient feeling, ancient city ruins and stone terraces, thousands of years of civilisation and a continuity there of the land, the diet, the culture. What did a few months matter in the building process. Admittedly, we experienced some frustrations but as soon as progress recommenced and as Manos added new creative ideas into the design our positive feelings returned.

The month was proving to be good for progress with another batch of photos providing further evidence of "good works." The plasterers had been in attendance – the new wall and the inside of the tiny bathroom had received a coat of grey rendering as had the ceiling below the new terrace. The roof outside had also received some attention with a smooth new finish in concrete to the edge of the tiled roof tidying up where the tiles abutted the roof terrace.

Within a few days we were updated with more progress downstairs. The new curved bathroom wall had been coated with gleaming, smooth white plaster giving a dramatic contrast with the grey and honey coloured stone walls. The staircase wound around this new wall and had become a small space in it's own right. Each progress update caused some jubilation at a distance of almost two thousand miles from the actual scene of the activity. Were we really seeing the completion of the house – at last? Progress continued through February – Manos had promised that the completion of the pointing and plastering would be followed by the installation of the doors and windows. We had last seen photos of these stacked up in the workshop having been painted about a month before Christmas. True to the plan, this was the

177

next development for the house. The pictures showed the new grey painted windows and shutters installed into
the rough multicoloured stone walls. Manolis had retained the original bendy rough wood lintels which provided a strong contrast to the smooth regular new windows.

All of a sudden the photos were showing a house, not a building site. The windows made a real difference and we carefully studied the smallest details. Yes, the glass had been put in and the window handles were an interesting bronze colour. Closer scrutiny revealed that there was a keyhole in the front door – with a key ! This was progress but before we got too carried away we had to remind ourselves that the windows were just "pegged" in – presumably waiting for the window sills and pictures showed coils of wire poking out of the various switch and socket holes. The stairs still had temporary treads and there were no floor boards yet on the first floor but still the new windows looked great and we were seeing real progress. Later the same day there was another update this time it showed pictures of the outside of the house. The windows still looked great against the newly cleaned and re-pointed stone walls. The most reassuring aspect to us was the house looked not too dissimilar from the original photos taken that first day we had see the house. The renovation work had not substantially altered the appearance which was exactly our intention. Manos had really met the brief and the original character and dignity of the old building had been preserved. Maybe the interior would be a different matter but we were picturing a tasteful blend of old and new with the beautiful colours of the stones and original timbers used for lintels and roof beams combining with the new windows and shutters and distressed new metalwork of the reinforcing frame and spiral stairs. We hoped that we would be witnessing this pleasant contrast in the near future or at least before our spring visit when we planned, at last, to stay in the house.
The pictures of the exterior also revealed details of other progress, the rain gutter in the front was in place and a down-pipe had been installed though closer examination revealed they still needed a "dog leg" pipe to connect them. In the pictures, although the sky was grey both sides of the house were bordered with rampant blooms of geraniums, in full flower in February!
An email from Manos followed the photo updates and the best news

was that the Building inspector had signed off the outside works. Given the difficulty in agreeing the little roof terrace in the first place this was a huge relief although I hadn't really contemplated what would happen if the works had not been agreed. The email also outlined the next steps that were planned. We had agreed that the treads of the staircase should be made out of the same stones we were to use on the ground floor, Manos confirmed this- accompanied by an alarming weather update:-

"Very cold here, with snow.
The whitish steps of stone at the staircase, vertical and horizontal (except for the 5 top verticals which will be in glass) and the gray phestos stone for the door and windows sills, are ready.
They will be located as soon as it stops raining.
The hatch and the flap of the staircase contact are under preparation.
Best wishes for a nice weekend"
M.

Shortly after this email we received a request to think about the bathroom. The options were really between pressed cement or tiling and if tiling what sort. We were confident that tiling would be our preferred choice but as usual this opened up yet more options. What sort of tiles, what colours, would the floor be the same as the walls and the usual worry about the small space and light. It needed some consideration.

The "flap of the staircase" that Manos referred to was another matter. Throughout the project the architect had offered some design touches that we had resisted. On occasions we thought he was joking or at the very least testing our limits. There had been the proposed glass sandwich door to the bathroom with the cavity filled with ping pong balls, also the creation of the whole sun terrace as well as the treads of the spiral stairs in glass. These had both been resisted but we had relented when he proposed "memory flaps" up the side of the stairs. The staircase had been constructed as a metal skeleton over the planned bathroom and the creation of the new bathroom wall on one side of the staircase had still left a gap between the stairs and the old stone walls at the other side. This could be filled with wood or plaster but as there could be some flexing of the stairs Manos proposed using metal to give greater rigidity. This would allow one of his new creative ideas –"memory flaps." These were described as narrow metal troughs alongside the stair treads that could be filled with items collected when out – "you know, pebbles, polished glass from the beach, driftwood, dried flowers – memories of your walks." – we acceded, why not.

We emailed back some ideas for the bathroom tiling:

Dear Manos

Some pictures from Gaudi buildings -we wondered whether there could be a link between the white stone chosen for the main ground floor room and possible mosaic finish in white and grey in the bathroom - with perhaps a little colour in it - and maybe a similar theme to the pictures with an irregular "track' of broken mosaic tile leading out into the room -similar to the pictures. What do you think?

The bathroom will need to be light tile mosaic - whites and greys mainly ?

He replied that he would pass the ideas to the resident artist, Irini who would come up with some ideas.

Early March saw an update with the windows firmly in place with the grey phestos stone window sills installed cleanly below each one – this gave a clean uniform edge against the multicoloured, irregular stones of the wall but really finished off the windows. Each update was welcomed as a small step towards completion; it had been a long process. Around this time I decided that I would construct a list of outstanding works to be completed. This was in an attempt to reassure me of how much had been done and how little was left to be done.

Outstanding works – March 2009

Clean steelworks
Steels to stairs
S/s Drain metals
Roof hatch
Terrace window
Finish gutter
Floor tiles
Bathroom walls
Stair treads and backs
Electricity plug and switches & Fuse Box
sockets for w/m & fridge?

Floor boards upstairs
Glass panels in floor
Bathroom Door
Instal sink
Install WC
Shower
W/m connections
Expelair fan

Kitchen?
sink unit /work top kitchen
Air con unit?

The last three items were outside the scaled back contract but Manos had talked with us about a kitchen design when we were there the previous summer. The good news was that the whole list easily fitted on an A4 sheet of paper so it did have the desired effect of cheering me up. We had also been compiling a file of photos of the works and occasional examinations of this reassured me how much had been achieved. From the very beginning I had described the house as a pile of stones, in a pretty village with an amazing view. The building process had confirmed this and at various times it had been reduced to the four stone walls which themselves were blasted back to their constituent stones. The ground floor had been dug up, through two and a half metres of solid bedrock and the roof, roof timbers, first floor and windows and doors were all removed! The new drains and water tanks had been created. Two new windows were opened up and a large injection of metal framework had created the first floor, new roof terrace and the two staircases. A number of niches had been put into the thick stone walls along with the necessary reinforcements and within the walls themselves all the electrics and pipeworks had been hidden. Before the roof had gone back on; re-using some of the old roof joists, the top of the walls were re-inforced with concrete beams. The poor old house was subjected to the indignity of being pressure washed inside and out before all the cracks and holes in the walls were repointed. Now, with the roof back on, this time securely fixed in place and weather-tight, a new roof –terrace, new windows, this time with glass in and a front door which looked like it fitted securely the old house was ready to face the world after it's trauma of renovation. The remaining works were virtually all internal ones.

The 'Planned' Hatch

We were planning to return to Crete in mid-May and intended to stay in the house; camping if necessary, so it seemed time to get some view of progress and what was to happen next. An email to Manos produced a reply about the works that were planned. It appeared that there was once again a delay due to scheduling. The rather complex design for the hatch to the roof terrace had been reconsidered mostly through concerns about it being made water-tight. The redesign had led to a delay in the Iron man's work so Manos was now scheduling the stonemason to come and lay the stone floor downstairs and construct the stone treads on the stairs. The floor and stairs would then need to be protected while the Iron man installed the hatch and put in the metal covers for the drains and pumps.

13 march

I have been waiting for the iron man to finish the hatch (which we have severely modified and I will explain this to you later on) so that the stone staircase and the stone floor will be located and not damaged by the iron man. We have changed this program because the iron man is delaying since I have requested the modification. So Monday they will start locating the stone staircase and floor and will protect it for the iron man to continue.

Now the hatch. It is no longer two pieces, but one piece, because we could not be sure about resolving the water insulation. So the staircase pole is cut and there is a central bar at the hatch based also on the central pole except of the surrounding.

The glass initially proposed was not giving enough guarantee, so I have found these glass tiles (pls check the uploaded photo). So the hatch is one piece, opening aided by electrically operated lever (you can see this in the middle). All these pieces, except some details, have been ordered and are here. The whole thing is operated with a remote control. The colour is a natural aluminium colour, which you can see in the picture. .

WC: We have the normal hanging toilet is 56 cms; I have found a shorter version of it which is only 48 cms. I think these 8 cms are quite important.

Warm regards Manos

17 march

I have ordered the pine wood wooden planks for the mezzanine. My question to you is - What do you want to see from the bottom part of this floor? Should these be protected , or painted ?How do you want the walk on part to be?

Dear Manolis
Thanks for the information about the floor.
The underneath could be plain wood if this is as light as the planks under the first floor roof. They should be protected but clear varnish or seal is fine.
For the top to be walked on - a similar seal perhaps with a whitish slight liming effect to lighten - how does that sound?
We confirm as discussed on the phone that the glass plates in the floor can be clear
Thanks

20/3

The white stone steps have been located and I think they look nice. They have been protected with a protection liquid and covered. The cement layer in the room to accept the stone tiles is ready - taking care to locate a frame of vertical marble strip around the 3 openings so that the 3 stainless recessed (to accept the stone) steel covers can be prepared and inserted by the iron man in a tight way.

I think you agree that the 3 covers should be stainless steel, so they will not get rust and they will be painting free. We wait that the cement layer gets dry so that the stone tiles can be located. The stone I have chosen at the end for the floor is whitish but a bit darker and match harder than the one used for the steps, natural looking, with some small cavities and not a precise border. Their size is 20 cm X 40 cm.

The questions here are : How wide would you like the pointing (gaps) between the stones? How would you like these to be laid?

Where is the bathroom door, a sill in white stone like the one of the staircase has to be located so that after that point the bathroom floor is recessing for the water to be contained.

The long window all along the gap is ready. I have opted for iroko wood and not pine wood in order to have a higher guarantee about the water proofing since iroko been an African heavy wood behaves better than pine wood regarding dilatation, cracks etc . Iroko is dark brown. My question here is: would you like that to be only transparent varnished /protected or painted in the grey colour of the other doors and windows? Sorry if I do not upload photos but in both my visits I had forgotten to insert the memory card in the camera! Getting older....

Warm regards from a very warm and sunny Crete.

M

Dear Manos
Thanks for the information about the floor.
The underneath could be plain wood if this is as light as the planks under the first floor roof. They should be protected but clear varnish or seal is fine.
For the top to be walked on a similar seal perhaps with a whitish slight liming effect to lighten- how does that sound?
We confirm as discussed on the phone that the glass plates in the floor can be clear
Thanks

30/3 This is the way I was thinking to lay the stone tiles with ½ cm pointing gap, whitish.Tomorrow we are applying on all iron surfaces

RUSTABIL

Warm regards

The electrician has proceeded cabling and creating new line for the hatch. I would like to know which are the lights you want me to locate and which are the ones you would eventually like to leave empty so that you could personally decide on these. The black smith was at the house today in order to

1.   Proceed towards covering the gap between staircase and wall over bathroom

2.   Fix laterally spiral staircase so that it is firm.

3.   Create the frame for the glass to be inserted in wooden floor.

4.   The hatch seems to be at a good point.......

I have to find the time to go together with tiller and create the bathroom walls tiling . I have chosen some colours of which there is tiles availability and would like to play with these...you can see the photo and tell me what do you think. Obviously Irini is not available.......The floor is here, painted, and will be located as soon as the frame for glass is located. Warm regards

P.S. Could I have a firm date of your arrival?

We were looking forward to the first trip of the year. Back in the winter progress had been good on the house and it seemed likely when I booked the plane tickets in January that May would see us staying in the house for the first time. At the end of April, less than three weeks from our return to the island, this option looked distinctly less likely.

The hatch to the roof terrace still appeared not to have been installed, there were no floorboards to the first floor, a recent photo had shown the bathroom window to be sitting in a niche and the bathroom had not been tiled or had any of the fittings installed. On top of this the final fittings of electrics and plumbing would involve the two most elusive workers on the whole project. We had assumed that we would be camping in the house as we had no furniture and hadn't agreed any kitchen layout. The plan was to take out a small electric hob, we already had a coffee maker there in the luggage in store. Sleeping would be on a camping airbed – not yet bought. All of these plans required operational plumbing and electrics and a set of floor boards! Further progress was eagerly awaited by us

Returning

A day time flight returned us to the island; the temperature rose some ten degrees from the Sussex we had left behind and was a pleasant high twenties. After collecting the hire car at the airport we drove east on the new national road, commenting on the flowering shrubs lining the road and the very green looking olive groves. In the distance there was still a little snow on the mountain tops but roadside vendors were selling large bags of potatos and bunches of small bananas. Time away allowed one to forget what a country of contrasts Crete was. Within an hour we were parking in the hill village where we borrowed the completed house from the architect and unpacking more luggage than normal because of our "camping ambition." We were met by the estate agent delivering clean linen for us. After exchanging greetings and news we arranged to go to the office to catch up with Manos – he was seeing another client but said he would meet us in twenty minutes time at the restaurant up the road; it was one of our favourites with views over the marina and the bay from an airy terrace sheltered under a canopy and screened by trees. We caught up with family news with the owners who were combing catering and social duties with after school child-care for their energetic children. Manos arrived in good spirits and joined us for something to eat and drink. He said the projects work was still busy for the business but the estate agency had quietened down over the winter. He then presented us with the key to the house – it was fixed with a glossy red key holder with a little white light. It was good to see him again and we couldn't wait to see the progress on the house. Before setting off to the village and our house we collected the bags of clothes that had been in the architectural store room through the winter. Theoretically this was arranged so that we travelled lighter but we seemed to be accumulating larger and larger wardrobes in Crete. Half an hour later we were walking through the village down to our house with eager anticipation to see first hand the work we had been following so keenly on the internet through the winter and earlier part of the year.

We were not disappointed. The newly cleaned stone walls were beautiful and the grey-painted shutters and door blended well with the old stones. After opening the front door with the flash new door key we

187

saw the tiled floor and the new wall and door to create the bathroom. We opened the shutters on the new window downstairs to let more light in. It was hard to work out what features we had seen before and which ones we had committed to memory from the photos Manos had been posting on the project picture web-site. We were shown around with some modest pride by Manos –"here is the tiling...are you sure you like it?" We had seen the pictures and had made a request for a "Gaudiesque" effect but in real life any doubts we had soon went away. Yes, they were striking which was exactly the phrase I had first used to him after seeing the photos. At that time he had said "Ah –you don't like the tiling!" We once again assured him and realized that the three of us were standing in the bathroom that we were all worried about the size. It can't be too small as we were all in it. Though as Manos pointed out, the wc and sink hadn't been installed yet. The architect's creativity was still in full flight –" I have been thinking that there is a small space at the side of the stairs that would lend themselves to a frosted glass panel that would let some light into the bathroom void area. It would create a small light well with light from the glass roof hatch –what do you think?" We liked the idea and readily agreed. There were also glass plates to put on the backs of some of the stairs for the same reason. We felt confident this would be an interesting bathroom but the main question was –when would it be functional?

Going through the rest of the house there was a lot of new works to examine. We had got used to this process following a familiar pattern with Manos both on-site and over the phone. We would say how de-lighted we were would some new addition or piece of building work and he would modestly say it was simple or that the work could have been improved with more room or better craftsmen or by manufacture in Athens or Italy. Any hesitation on our part was met defensively –"You don't like it. We must change it – it is your house – what colour/size/pattern etc etc." We looked at the shiny new fuse box so different from the jumble of boxes at home under the stairs in Sussex. It's uni-form lines of neat little fuses some with red or green little lights twin-kling behind a neat perspex door fitted into a small niche just inside the house –"You don't like it... you would prefer a grey door to match the woodwork? I will get it changed !" We both protested."It's fine – really. You should see our fuses back home - antiquated!"

"You want the box to be hidden? The carpenter could make a small wooden cupboard to disguise it – would you prefer that?"

"No , no it's lovely, really – we love it –really modern and functional-does it work?"

"Ah, the electrician will connect it all tomorrow – the lighting is not on yet "– then, darkly, "don't touch any loose wires." Downstairs was a little congested with the three of us in an already small space that doubled as a resting place for the builders tools, tile cutters, tool box-es, unused wiring materials, tiles and plumbing materials as well as some of the old shutters and some new metal plates as well as rubbish dump for packing and discarded materials. I was very careful not to touch any loose wires. Because of his evidence of activity (which we were anxious to not inhibit) it was difficult to see the new tiles on the ground floor. We liked what we could see – large book sized light coloured stone plates, slightly irregular with a textured surface. The floor was also 'punctuated" with some large holes, some with metal plates over, partially tiled, some more alarmingly open –another, next to the new staircase looked dark and deep – "that is to the septic tank –it's deep " said Manos –" let's look upstairs."

We needed no second bidding but already knew from the view downstairs through the steel framework to the ceiling of upstairs that the first floor was somewhat conceptual at this stage. In fact, upstairs was more dangerous than the ground floor. The staircase looked good with stone treads over the metal framework; it also felt solid but progress ended quickly as we all three gathered on the top of the stairs looking across the first floor room. The metalwork frame was still without floorboards and as a result needed circus skills to negotiate in full. I restricted myself to walking across a scaffolding plank to the spiral staircase leading up to the roof terrace – Manos quickly followed –"Don't go on the terrace! Another coat of insulation was placed there this morning and you shouldn't walk on it yet."

Sure enough the terrace was now a glossy grey coat , looking like a bumper layer of putty. Empty it was possible to imagine a table and seating for six of us, dining under the stars….one day. Back in the real world Manos showed me where the terrace walling had been raised and all re-pointed in white mortar. Reluctantly, he waved at the opening to the terrace, where we were standing at the top of the spiral stairs. "This has been a nightmare!" he groaned. The metal man has not seen eye to eye with me – it is essential that it is made weathertight" …muttering to himself it was clear that this was not a suitable discussion for our first meeting there so I changed the subject and admired the new narrow, long set of windows onto the terrace; designed to bring light in and across the first floor ceiling.

For a change he agreed –"Yes, these have worked out well and allow in some nice diffused light." Unqualified approval - unusual.

Manos described the remaining works and his plans. A couple of additions were talked over. The building permit included a small balcony on the first floor outside the pair of small glass doors. We had removed it from the first building phase on cost grounds but Manos suggested completing it while the carpenter was still working at the house –we gave a quick agreement as we felt it would further open up the first floor room and allow a sea view without climbing up to the roof terrace. We were also beginning to think about furniture or at least storage and fittings. It was agreed that the new cavity created outside the bathroom wall would house the fridge freezer but there was extra room that could be a store cupboard. The other thing we noticed was the drop down the stair well from where the new first floor would be. We began to think that some screen or storage unit might be a practical safety feature. Talk about this was delayed until after the floor was installed. Of the planned works: the electrician would be coming the next day to finish the fuse panel. The plumber would connect the bathroom fittings once these were chosen – this could be done the next day. The carpenter would put in the first floor as soon as the messy work with the terrace coating and the roof hatch was complete. It still was all being held up by the hatch!

Additionally, there was all the cleaning, repainting and minor finishing jobs; in some cases repairing the damage done in the course of completion. This was probably the inevitable penalty of a cramped work-space. Looking around at everything to be done and the multiple "work in progress" areas in the house camping seemed optimistic – but, hey, this was only day one and we had another two weeks here yet! Back at the house in the hills we unpacked and renewed our acquaintances with the neighbours as well the clothes stored last year. A walk through the village and an early, by greek standards, supper in a village restaurant under the stars. Plenty of fresh cooked local recipes, a jug of cold wine – perfect!

The next day we were joined on the terrace for our breakfast by the ginger cat we had befriended on earlier stays. This time she was alone – last year she brought two young cats with her. After breakfast we drove to town to meet with the architect to choose bathroom fittings. We had a look around the town as our arranged meeting was later in the morning- it was bustling as usual; the marina car park near the office had introduced yet another revolutionary ticketing system but the cost remained at 3 euros all day! We strolled through town, said hello to a few people we recognised including the architect's mum in her shop. Put credit on our greek phone; browsed the bookshop and generally tried to get ourselves into a Cretan frame of mind for the drive with Manos to the bathroom emporium. In the office it was the usual mix of good taste – smart furniture, glossy magazines and individual objects. Manos only had one new challenge for us – he had selected some low energy downlighters to be fitted in the niches but showing one to us he pointed out that the light also came out sideways and that was not his vision for them – "we need to locate ones that only light down and are mains voltage – let me know the stockist or obtain a sample- here on the island or back in the UK." It appeared this was now our responsibility – still perhaps this would leave him freer to resolve the hatch dilemma. A new lady CAD designer was introduced to us and Manos's dog made her usual low key fuss with her friendly but doleful eyes. Cold drinks were offered but the usual clamour for Manos's attention from people, both residents and visitors plus the phones meant that Manos was keen to abandon the office we followed, as did his dog, out into the heat again and negotiated our way out of the town traffic to the bathroom fitting store. Once all the sunroof and several windows were open the minivan was left in the canine custody of the dog.

We had visited this builders merchant before; it was on the outskirts of town in a large building the front of which was a glass fronted show-room housing swish bathroom fittings, most of which were far too large for our purposes. There was also an impressive range of wall and floor tiles, some in glass like jewels. Manos breezed in and seemed to be known by the man behind one of the desks who waved before a younger woman engaged Manos in a machine gun speed greek con-versation. It transpired she was to show us the small wash basin and taps he had selected for the small wet-room in our house; we were led upstairs to view these. This part of the visit was quite straightforward but it was soon to degenerate into typical Manos inspired chaos. As far as we could tell there was some enquiry from Manos about an order for a WC and whether they had papers which described the dimen-sions. The conversation became more heated with the woman employ-ing elaborate hand gestures towards the wc's on display. After more low key greek shouting the three of us were led back downstairs to the office where a close examination of the paper filing system as well as scrutiny of a pc monitor took place. This must have been quite stress-ful as the guy came in from the outside desk to help; although his help seemed restricted to accepting the offer of one of Manos's strong greek architectural cigarettes which they both smoked whilst reviewing some of the paper – upside down. Gathering up two steel tape mea-sures we all reassembled upstairs and started measuring the wc's. Th e distance out from the wall seemed the key measurement. Unfortu-nately some of these measurements needed to be compared with the paper records - still downstairs; fortunately the building was air-condi-tioned!

When we trailed once more upstairs we were led through another door to be confronted by a version of the closing sequence to the first Indi-ana Jones film – the scene where the crated ark is stored away in a vast warehouse of other crates. I exaggerate but only slightly - the space was about ten times larger than the showroom and full of crates and large cardboard boxes. Manos and the woman scuttled down the aisles examining the greek writing and numbers in some quest to lo-cate a particular item. We hung around as confused by-standers until some consensus had been arrived at over whether they had found what they were looking for. We reconvened downstairs in the office, relieved to see the smoking hadn't allowed the paper-work to combust. After a brief conversation Manos announced it was time to go and the wc had been selected – did we want to try it. Sitting in my shorts on a wc in the mercifully quiet showroom certainly didn't figure as one of my least embarrassing experiences – still we had apparently save some 150 euros over a previously identified compact one – we were a bit mystified but reassured by Manos who stated that the plumber could now proceed. Later the same day two events occurred. We were able to switch on the lights in the house for the first time; Greek tv announced the country's first case of Mexican swine flu'- the events were unconnected as far as we were aware.

Wednesday found us up early shopping near the harbour at the weekly market. It wasn't long before I had to restrain S –"Stop, I don't think I can carry anymore! How much have we spent?" Apparently, less than ten euros and that included a 4 euro jar of honey; we had a large bag of mixed sweet pepper, artichokes, aubergines, big beef tomatoes, a big bag of beautiful yellow potatoes and plenty of other things. After dropping the supplies back at the village house we drove over to review building progress. Manos was already there talking to the back of the plumber who was working on the pumps in the cavities under the ground floor. Most of this system seemed quite mysterious to me but it seemed to be one of those areas just to trust the experts. The plumbing was most effective in the loan house so evidence appeared to be supportive of this action. The plumber broke off to shake hands and lead us into the tiny bathroom where- amazingly- the wc was plumbed in – was this the one that was the subject of so much discussion only yesterday! We agreed the positions for the basin and shower and diplomatically withdrew to let them get on with it. Later that day whilst trying to drive to a local viewpoint we came across an abandoned village and we couldn't help noticing that most of the houses resembled ours during the last visit – walls of bare stone, no roofs, gaping holes instead of shutters – there had been progress on the project- slow progress but progress nevertheless. That evening we arranged a visit to the south of the island for later in the week to meet up with an old friend who was now the proud owner of a building plot full of stones with spectacular views. At least it would allow the "architectonis" and the builders to make progress or conduct convoluted discussions with local builders merchants without our assistance.

A Trip to the South

The evening before our planned trip the architect called to see if we would be at the house the following morning to see the installation of the hatch. We felt that this was a significant step so we readily agreed but when we arrived up at the house there was no sign of Manos. The metal man and his assistant were both there wresting with a large, shiny silver frame up on the roof terrace – the infamous "Hatch." We said our "hello's" and retreated to the local kefenion and phoned Manos. "Have we missed you – or should we wait for you?" His voice betrayed his mood – "I am depressed about the hatch – it is difficult, it must be watertight and let in light – I am still not sure about the design. I have told them to fit it anyway – we will have to see. You have your trip to the south and we will on your return –drive safely!"

We chatted with Maria in the kefenion; noticing for the first time a May garland, now dried, hanging in her doorway. We also admired a neighbour's new dog and chatted to the owners but knew we needed to leave if we were to complete the journey in the morning. With Maria's goodbyes echoing in our ears and here parting gift of a fresh pear we set off. The trip would take us along the north coast past the airport and skirting the capital we would then strike south through the mountains. It should take us up to three hours although we had noticed how much the Cretan roads had improved in recent years. The drive west was familiar to us from regular trips to Heraklion and to the airport. It was still a scenic route with the roadsides lined with large flowering shrubs, bright against the distant backdrop of the mountains. The normal route was briefly interrupted by a diversion back onto one of the old roads as a result of a dramatic rockfall near one of the monasteries. The traffic built up near the airport and only thinned out once we had negotiated the outskirts of the capital and turned south where the road initially followed the valley floor before climbing into the mountains. Buildings started to thin out with housing being replaced by new metal and glass retail buildings and car showrooms. Eventually this gave way to fertile farmland with some landscapes being reminiscent of Italy and France with tall plane trees and fields of vines. The Cretans put their own touch to the vineyards where they had avoided the bother of wires and training- letting the vines grow more naturally near the ground. We broke the journey after a couple of hours for cold drinks, the outside temperature had risen into to the thirties and the streets of the towns and villages seemed dustier than in the north. The directions from Dave had been accurate and it wasn't long before we met up with him- on his bike! We did a little fresh food shopping in the village he was staying in and then enjoyed a welcome lunch in the shade of the garden. He was interested to hear of the building progress at our house having seen it in it's "raw state" the year we had bought it. His own project was a building plot bought the previous year on a hill-top overlooking the village with views of the mountains as well as to the sea to the south – and who knows - on a clear day – to Africa. After lunch we did the usual "mad dog and Englishman " thing, fortified by chilled wine, of walking out in the full glare of the sun to view the building plot. Thankfully, there was some shade under a large, mature olive tree and it was here that we heard Dave's plans for the house and garden on the site. It was good to talk with someone else who saw a house on the island as part of their life; different to locals or people who had completely relocated there. We know that two homes would be a luxury but see it as the best solution for us.

That evening we ate a late supper in a local restaurant – very friendly and family run with Cretan recipes using fresh ingredients. The restaurant was busy with people celebrating the end of the week – noisy with conversations in Greek, German and Italian as well as English. Suddenly, conversation on the terrace ceased as we all stared as a large ghostly winged figure swooped into the square below. It took us a short time to realise it was a large white owl; it's size magnified by the glare of the light from the restaurant and the street. Very Cretan – a country where you can nature watch whilst having supper. The next day we had a drive out to a cliff side monastery – deserted but still used for retreats. The stone cells were cool out of the hot sun and in some cases equipped with cooking utensils, oil lamps and drinks - including wine and beer! The views down the steep valley towards the coast were stunning but the stillness of the cells themselves were quite moving. Lunch was taken at a fish restaurant already, down at the coast. Earlier in the week he had warned the lady owner that he planned to bring some friends over for a meal who, unlike him, were not vegetarians. The owner welcomed us and supplemented our fish meal order with a small starter of liver pieces in a rich herb and tomato sauce - provided gratis! We had enjoyed our trip to another part of the island but the time had come to take our leave and return to the north and meet up with some other friends that evening. We wished Dave good luck with his own Cretan project and took to the road.

We arrived back up in our village in the early evening – still warm but some cooling in the deeper shadows in the narrow streets. There was progress at the house! The metal hatch was installed but it still lacked glass. The bathroom was now equipped with a sink, taps and shower – but the water was still switched off – we wisely resisted the urge to turn on the water and try it. There was a lull in progress and discussions for a couple of days – Manos was ill. We amused ourselves with days out and showing two friends who were in Crete for the first time around the island including the house (or more correctly, the building site.) The next time we met the architect he was back to his normal energy levels. He rushed up to us in the café around the corner from the office where we were having lunch with the two friends – "It is a catastrophe!!" he exclaimed – before he remembered his manners and said hello and allowed me to carry out some brief introductions. "It is the hatch –I have been there and –Oh, I don't know –the metal man – I don't think it's right – it has to be weather tight – the glass - Oh it's all too difficult ……" his voice trailed off, he rolled his sad brown eyes over the top of his designer glasses and stretched out both his arms in a resigned shrug. I suggested he stayed for lunch or a drink with us but now with quick goodbyes and a volley of greek at the owners he was gone. He had been described already to our friends who had seen

second hand the process of renovation at a distance when we were all in Sussex. We shrugged – "well he is a great architect –just a bit of a personality!"

A few days later on our next site visit to the house we found that the glass man had paid a visit and put the plates of frosted glass at the back of the stair treads above the bathroom. This was part of the plans to bring light down through the building. The more exciting part of this was also underway. There were to be four large sheets of plate glass set in the floorboards on the first floor and they had been installed. They looked rather surreal – like a four pane window lying on the floor- the steel framework still bare, awaiting the floorboards. It was all really beginning to take shape. We were elated as so many of the design features that had been the subject of hours of discussion by phone, email as well as face to face, were appearing in front of our eyes. These were design details that had seemed rather remote all the time Albanian stonemasons were demolishing and rebuilding stone walls and creating niches. The dusty stone walls, open to the sky, did not at that stage seem to lend themselves to creations in glass and stained wood. We were pleased that stage in the works was now behind us, although Manos had mentioned only the previous week that he had hoarded a supply of matching stone in case more was required and there was mention of a small bed for planting a vine in the street, although, mysteriously this was a matter he suggested needed referral to the "village" for approval. I decided that it would be best for him to manage that particular matter when we arrived at it. We took time out on the Saturday to leave early to drive to Sitia in the east where on some previous visits we had found a few interesting shops that we thought would be of interest when we were nearer furnishing the house – we were starting to think that point had at last arrived. There was also Manos's newly commissioned search for low voltage niche lights. The drive was pleasant, the roads quiet, smoother than the worn out surfaces of the hard-pressed British road network and the scenery spectacular. We arrived and parked near the harbour and fortified ourselves with iced coffees. The town had a grid of streets of small shops leading up the hill from the harbour and we particularly remembered a kitchenware and glass shop, a large ironmongers/ electrical shop, as well as several linen shops. The main question was exactly where they were but at least the search would be interesting. The linen and kitchenware shops were found reasonably quickly but the electrical shop proved more elusive – but in the process we stumbled across a nice bookshop, several clothes shops and an interesting coffee supplier. At last we found the electrical emporium and it was a worthwhile find as they were able to provide exactly the sort of niche downlighters that Manos had specified – two samples were bought and a stock number written on a card for future orders – a success. Lunch at a harbour side restaurant was our reward.

In the afternoon, rather than drive back by a direct route to the east we left Sitia by a road to the south and climbed over a mountain range until at last we could see the Libyan sea glinting in the distance beyond the south coast of the island. This end of the island is sparsely populated but the roads were good and occasionally they pass through a small hamlet or past a farmhouse or well kept church, apparently in the middle of nowhere. On the south coast itself there are recent examples of ambitious resort hotel developments but such schemes are outnumbered by large agro-industrial developments of acres of poly-tunnels growing tropical fruits which are reputed to make the area one of the richest in the whole of Greece. The only evidence of this seems to be the incidence of new car dealers, their large, flashy cars and the occasional lavish new villa. We stopped at Makrigialos, a pretty fishing harbour with a narrow sandy beach and seaside holiday cottages and small bars and restaurants. The cold drinks and ice creams were most welcome. A drive back along the south coast, skirting Ierapetra and a drive back to the north coast punctuated by a swim brought us to our temporary home. Supper out with friends that evening completed a busy day.

We were back up at the house early the next morning to meet with Manos and the carpenter who was installing the floor boards; fitting them around the new glass panel between the ground and the first floor. This relatively straightforward task was made more difficult by the structure of the house: the boards had to be screwed to the metal beam "lattice work" and carefully fitted between the irregular stone walls and the new glass plate. The size of the house also meant that each board was being taken outside to be sawn to size- this took place in our narrow street where careful manipulation of the four metre long boards was required to get them out and back into the house again. We thought the lack of space meant that it was best to leave Manos, the carpenter and his assistant to get on with the job but before we left we were asked for our opinion on the exact shade of whitening to be used to colour wash the floor once it was laid. These seemed real points of detail and finish that confirmed that we were at last reaching the completion stages of the project. More excitingly we realised that by the end of the day we would at last be able to walk around in the first floor room – something that had been impossible for some months since the old floor had been removed. Any time up there even to just take photos had required rudimentary circus skills- goodness knows what it had been like to complete any actual work! We had a morning drink at Maria's and told her about recent progress. "Soon you will be moving in to live here" she told us in greek. The rest of the day we had a leisurely Sunday lunch on the terrace of a favourite restaurant followed by a swim. By that time it was late afternoon and the little house was quiet and locked up again. We opened the door, there was a strong smell of new wood and sawdust. For the first time we could get the scale of the house. Downstairs still had abandoned tools and building materials covering the floor. Some of the floor hatches were still up again making our movement difficult but we were able at last to gauge the amount of light available to us downstairs even though it was still a building site. Upstairs, once we removed our shoes we were able to walk around. There was plenty of light coming through the roof hatch and the long window on the terrace. When we opened the two sets of shutters on the windows there was even more light. The boards had been screwed to the metal floor frame and the holes were filled with some kind of mastic; tomorrow they would be painted with the whitening paint wash. Today had seen a real milestone passed with us being able to walk around the first floor on proper floorboards. We looked forward to more being finished in the coming days and decided to swap our return flights for tickets a week later to see as much progress as possible.

We used the rest of the week as a holiday, seeing friends, walks, swimming, some shopping with the opportunity to look at essentials for the house. The visits up to the house were rewarded with signs of progress but they were mostly finishing touches. The paint wash on the first floor made that room lighter. The plumber appeared to have completed the bathroom with shiny new shower fittings and connections under the stairs for a washing machine. The water remained turned off with a visit from the metal man to redo the floor hatches;

which would then need retiling. Alarmingly, there was still no glass in the hatch and any attempt at hurrying the architect to resolve this only resulted in his really depressed expression, mutterings about the metal man and glaziers in general and a change of topic of conversation. By Thursday we remembered that we had talked about making a complete set of measurements of the house to help with planning storage and furniture but once that task was completed another event that day conspired to change our lives.

An Acccident

It was early evening and we were back at the village house that had been kindly loaned to us by the architect. I had taken something upstairs, washing I think, to rinse on the terrace and hang out. Coming back down the stone staircase, I guess with wet bare feet I found myself losing my footing. I arrived at the foot of the stairs on my back. The next thing I heard was "Can you hear me?" and being shaken! Opening my eyes was like a scene from a comic – as I moved my head around I was seeing stars – and my right leg and bum hurt like hell! I had been unconscious for no more than twenty or thirty seconds but this seemed a lifetime to Swho was now reluctant to try and haul me to my feet or at least to my knees! With instructions not to move she ran round the corner to a neighbour's house. I wasn't sure I could! She soon arrived back with Matt, a neighbour, and his Mum and I was slowly raised to a seating position but I was still seeing stars. Cautiously, I answered questions - did I feel sick? Could I focus my eyes? Could I rotate my head? Move my leg; wiggle my toes. All seemed well but a large bump was rising on my head and the stars at last, went away. Nothing seemed to be broken and the offer of a trip to the hospital in the port was declined. An early night, a long sleep and a review of the position next morning was the plan. After a restless night that was mostly caused by my aching leg we decided a hospital visit would be a sensible precaution. My leg was more painful than my head, with the bump having shrunk away. I hobbled into the general hospital reception where we were directed to a general waiting area. After a short time we realised there was an appointment system in operation and fearing we could be there several hours waiting our turn I suggested ringing Manos for advice. We adjourned to a café opposite and made the call.

His concern was immediate – "drive Geoff over here straightaway; I will call my doctor and get him to see you as soon as possible." It sounded a good offer and within the hour after an iced frappe at the office we were in the doctor's waiting room. After a short wait we were called in. "Hello, I am George and Manos has told me about the incident. Where is the pain at the moment?" Dr George carried out a thorough series of tests and conducted a detailed cross examination with questions about the fall as well as my general health. He even put out his cigarette in the ash-tray on his desk and resisted lighting another. Eventually, we both sat down and he offered his advice. There appeared not to be any serious repercussions from the fall. His tests had not revealed any signs of neurological effects. He outlined the sort of things I should watch for; including nausea, balance problems, eyesight changes etc. He recommended visiting my doctor back in England in a week's time.

Reassured, I asked if there were any changes I should make. He suggested I should avoid strenuous exercise, (I do anyway!) and should avoid excessive drinking but as I was on holiday and it was hot – social drinking was ok. By this, he elaborated, he meant a glass or two of wine with my evening meal should be ok! As an afterthought he added that social smoking should be ok as well as the flight home next week! If I had any concerns I should call him again. We returned back to the office feeling relieved and relayed the information to Manos. We laughed about the "social drinking and smoking" and Manos offered me one of his high strength cigarettes - I readily refused. As an alternative he suggested lunch – his treat out of guilt about the stairs- despite me reassuring him it was only my own fault that the fall had taken place. A welcome long lunch was taken under trees at a restaurant near the office and apparently owned by the mother of our electrician. Manos was now also feeling delicate and arriving at the restaurant announced to the owner, in a stage whisper, "I have diarrhea, what do you recommend?" I am certain that in England that same request would have been met with something like "I recommend you eat somewhere else!" Thankfully, we were the first customers and the owner brought a plate of two fried eggs for Manos before serving large helpings of mixed mezedas to the three of us. I drank a soft drink resisting the recommended "social drinking" while Manos fortified by the eggs ate at least half the mezedas and drank a couple of cold beers. We chatted for an hour or two until I said I felt I needed a rest so we returned to the house. Manos, I hope, went back to the office to lie down as well.

Sunday morning was spent agreeing the outstanding list of works to be completed with Manos. The main items that were obstructing this was the hatch and the metal hatch covers on the ground floor. Manos was also in creative mode this morning – "what about a folding bed attached to the metalwork. It would give you much more flexibility up-stairs. I know somewhere in town that can have sprung mattresses made up to any size- not expensive. I will give you directions." In the bathroom he proposed using the metal upright as a spine for some small shelving that would be useful storage. Up on the roof we dis-cussed the necessity for shade. We had brought a large white triangu-lar canvas sail from England. We asked if anything could be done with this. We stretched it out; it would need some uprights to suspend it from. "Leave it with me. I'll see what can be done with it." The prob-lems with the hatches, the roof one and the ground floor hatches had kept downstairs as a building site. In this state even though we had taken measurements there had been limited opportunity to make deci-sions about any permanent arrangements for the kitchen units and seating which we knew we needed. The hope had been that we would camp in the house and give ourselves an idea of how much, or little, space there was and how we should split it. As a compromise we sug-gested to Manos that if his carpenter could make us a simple bench work surface, housing a sink, the taps could be fitted to the wall, then we could use it as a temporary kitchen until we felt we understood the space in the house for us to make some decisions on more permanent arrangements. This was readily agreed to - even suggested some stor-age below the work surface.

We agreed to meet again before leaving mid-week and we adjourned to a new restaurant that was quickly becoming our new favourite. We took a long lunch (again) on the first floor terrace in the restaurant created inside an old Carob factory. Carobs seem to be a wonder crop used as a chocolate substitute, as cattle fodder and as some mystery ingredient in photographic film production. The building has been beautifully restored with carefully selected fittings set against stone walls, lots of glass and pastel coloured furniture. I noticed that there were no pictures hung on the walls and cheekily asked the owner if they might be interested in some framed prints (the product of a re-cent spell at the print department of our local college.) The answer was typically Cretan –"why not, bring them with you next time and we'll look at them."

The following day we returned and ordered some wine. I showed the pictures to the owner who was complimentary but said he had thought he would leave the walls clear for the time being. He must have sensed my disappointment as he quickly asked me to bring the pictures with me – "we are going next door where we have a shop." We left the restaurant and just next door, down a couple of steps was a small shop and as my eyes adapted to the contrast between the bright sun outside and the comparatively subdued lighting within I saw a smiling dark haired lady sitting behind a carved polished wood desk. "This is my mother ' we exchanged a handshake "Geoff has some pictures for us to sell – where shall we put them?" The shop comprised two smallish rooms, stone walls and a cool tiled floor with sets of shelve and small tables on every wall. The stock was a mixture of beautiful coloured glass, racks of wine and local raki. Carved olive wood ornaments and kitchenware as well as the pretty coloured metal jugs used in restaurants for house wine. So near the start of the season it seemed very well stocked with little space for all five framed prints, each some two foot by eighteen inches. Dimitri was undeterred and started handing items off the shelves to me – once my arms were full I had to start putting stuff down on some of the other shelves. After several reshuffles and reducing some of the spacing between items we were left with a bare shelf – lit with spotlights and in a prime position facing the door. "We will put them here " he said decisively. I hoped his mother approved after all it was her shop. I needn't have worried she was smiling serenely and turned to attend to a customer who was making what appeared to be an impulse purchase of a large coloured glass piece for the princely sum of three hundred euros! Perhaps bringing the prints here would be a good move; then I remembered we had yet to discuss any commercial arrangements.

"Are you happy with the pictures here Geoff?" – "Yes, they look good – let's hope they will sell "I answered – " What are your normal arrangements for pricing with suppliers?" We quickly agreed on a simple arrangement – a fifty fifty profit split and a euros retail price per framed print with Dimitri, at my suggestion, having the option of discounting the price later in the season if they were unsold. As I folded up the large zip bag I had brought them in my pack of greeting cards with local photos fell out – "What are these – you do cards too?" "Yes, would you like some of these as well?" "Why not" he said positively. Let's go –your wine will be getting warm." I returned to the restaurant terrace where S. was enjoying the sun, the view and the wine! "You'd been gone ages – will they take any?" Smiling I was able to report that all five were on display in the shop next door together with the cards! On the strength of future revenue we ordered lunch and another carafe of wine –why not!

At home

We were away staying with friends in Wales towards the end of June when the next update arrived- just a photo of the spiral staircase and the hatch with the caption – "Glass for hatch has been located." This was good news as there had been much discussion about whether it would be one panel of glass or nine, plate glass or glass bricks or even in a fit of frustration, wood.

Dear Geoff

I hope you had a pleasant weekend. The glass for the hatch has been located. This week the iron man/glass man/electrician/me all go together to see how its working and what is needed.

I thought that would be a site meeting I would be happy to miss. Earlier in the process we had detected some fairly undisguised tensions between Manos and the 'Metal Man' and there had been some uncomplimentary comments about the Glassman. At one point Manos had told me that the 'Tile Man" thought they were all making too much fuss! Frustrated by the delay I had suggested, only half in jest, that the Tile man should be immediately commissioned to install a hatch of his own design- tiled or otherwise!

 I left my call to Manos until the end of the week and on the Friday morning had one of our usual style of conversations. It could not be described as being at total cross-purposes nor could it be thought of as entirely in tune. I opened the skirmish by asking whether the "hatch meeting" had concluded satisfactorily. He gave a guarded "Yes." I then asked him whether it had leaked at all and asked if he was satisfied with the seal. "Ah yes, it was fine for the hosepipe but here the winter rains will be unlike rain you have ever seen." "Ok, so we just hope it will be ok, then, but as far as it goes the house is now sealed and weather-tight." He then changed tack –"so, tell me when are you coming back again?" "Well, as we said – when the house is finished, and we can stay in it- let us know when that will be and then I can book flights." His reply was that we should tell him when we would be coming and the house would be finished by that date. I gave up and said we would talk about it here and contact him shortly, probably the next day.

The next day, after booking flights for the end of July, we called the office and relayed the dates also agreeing a few details to be finished. This visit did not place following a dramatic turn of events. Since the last visit in June I had suffered from painful headaches. Visits to our doctor and two subsequent trips to two casualty wards had only resulted in suggestions of migraine. After a rapid deterioration and a very frightening twenty four hours with the kind support of our friends Daryl and Martin I was to wake up in an intensive care unit in a neurology centre of a Sussex hospital. A surgical team had been called in and I had undergone an emergency and lifesaving operation. Delayed completion of a holiday home seemed an incidental matter. Once the haematoma was drained and following several days monitoring and a second brain scan I was released home for recuperation with stern instructions to take it very easy – no driving or flying for the immediate future. It appeared that the split second slip back in June and resulted in a very close call! After my dramatic hospital visit the need to recuperate pushed thoughts of the house project from my mind but there was a need to tell Manos that the planned visit in August would not be taking place. The latest emails had been some questions of detail that I had picked up while in hospital so these were briefly answered with an accompanying promise to call him in a few days without revealing the reason for this. I had been told to avoid any further drama and excitement and we concluded that conversation about the house, particularly with Manos usually involved a measure of both of these.

An update arrived via the photo website with some welcome progress. The floor tiles on the ground floor had been relaid which must mean the floor hatches had been re-installed. New stone inserts had been cut and fixed at he side of the stair treads and we could see that the air-condition unit had been installed, place neatly high up in the stairwell next to the spiral stairs. S. rang the office and broke the news to Helen and asked her when would be a good time to speak to Manos, knowing that he would be upset. An hour later a breathless and very concerned Manos was ringing us. "It is dreadful! How is Geoff? Will he be alright? I am so upset" Eventually, she asked if he would like to talk

210

to me. A plaintive Manos weakly enquired-" Can he speak?" We talked and I reassured him that the surgeon had said there was no reason that I should not make a full recovery as long as I took a period of taking things easy. In practical terms this meant postponing our planned visit for the following week.

"The house is almost ready – I will send you photos but are you sure that you will be ok – it is so tragic!" We broke the news of our abandoned trip to move into the house but emphasised that we would travel as soon as I received the all clear to. Conversation moved on to details of completed works and outstanding tasks – I felt an information overload and perceptively Manos must have sensed this as he said that it would be best to look at the photos and call with any questions or instructions for him. Exchanging best wishes we ended the call.

He was as good as his word and later the same day some more photos arrived showing that the fridge had been installed! There was also photos of a new doorbell, an outside light above the front door and a down lighter in one of the wall niches. Early evening I called Manos again to thank him for the photos and to check he was over the shock of my news. He sounded more composed but also promised to take some more photos that evening to show the lights in the house. Again, he wished me a speedy recovery and we looked forward to receiving this further update even though there was a growing sense of frustration at not being able to stay in the completed house. When we were able to look at the photos the next day we were truly delighted by them. The outside lights washed down the stones at the front of the house highlighting the contours and bringing out the honey coloured tones of the stones. The lights inside shone out through the open windows with the grey painted shutters and frames contrasting with the colour of the stones. The photos of the interior were equally rewarding. The same coloured stones with the wide light pointing between them looked wonderful with warm browns and yellows, relieved by some light greys. We had chosen some coloured light shades to use as four pendant lights to hang from the old wooden beams upstairs. These contrasted nicely with the sharper light of the downlighters and niche lights but their harshness was already tempered by the variety of colours in the stones of the walls. Manos had also prepared a small surprise for us by way of a ribbon of led lights forming an L shape along two walls. We had agreed with Manos to leave a gap between the walls and the floorboards on the first floor. He had eloquently described the floor as "floating' with light washing up and down the stone walls through the small gap. The led lights magnified this effect and looked very dramatic in the photos. There was also a practical aspect to the floating floor, meaning that the edge could be straight even though the wall surface was uneven. Another photo showed some expensive looking black box with a blue light on it – the title stated 'ups for the electric hatch mechanism' –very high tech, but perhaps essential if we didn't want to get stranded on the roof terrace. There were also picture of the stairs with the light from the bathroom shining through the frosted glass stair backs - illuminating the stairs, very theatrical. The whole look was close to our imagination – a blend of traditional and modern with interesting little design suprises. The final addition was the kitchen unit that the carpenter had made. There had been much discussion about the kitchen throughout the project but as the building details were finalised and we began to see more cretan houses and think about cretan recipes the options widened rather than narrowed. We concluded that we wanted to live in the house before finalising the kitchen so had asked Manos if a simple temporary kitchen bench could be made. This could have a simple sink inset, space for a freestanding hob and food preparation. The taps could be fixed on the wall and some storage made on a shelf below the work surface.

The phone rang early at home one morning – "Good morning, is it too early. I am up at your house and I am wondering about the plant for outside –what do you think a bougainvillea, a vine or a jasmine?" Well we must be nearly finished if he is thinking about planting shrubs! After a brief discussion we settled on a Jasmine; it would be more fragrant than a vine and less prickly stem than a bougainvillea. I once more expressed our gratitude and said how pleased we had been with the whole look of the house in the recent night pictures that he had sent us. He agreed that the lighting seemed to have enlarged the building, both inside and out. After he had gone we realised that today was the day we were to have flown out again but had to be cancelled because of my operation, no matter, the house would still be there for later visits.

The next contact from Manos was an on-line conversation one evening early in August. After asking about my post-op recovery progress he told us that the jasmine had been planted and was some two meters tall. We exchanged other text comments and then he became quite lyrical –"I have just finished a large project but it has not been as creative as your house. Your house is small, enlarged, unique and intelligent. I have enjoyed the project and working with you." This was good to hear because the three of us knew that the whole project had not been without it's frustrations for all of us but if we had got to this point and all felt so positive at the end of it then it had to be a good thing! He conclude by saying he would send a photo of the climbing jasmine and pictures of the inside after cleaning and we wished each other a good weekend. As promised a new set of pictures arrived with the first one showing the jasmine planted to the left of the front door and climbing three quarters of the way to the top of the door. Other photos were of the staircases after they had been cleaned as well as the new floorboards upstairs. There were also more images of details in the wet room with it's "shock' tiling which was still taking a little getting used to. The glass in the windows and floor panel looked clean as did the large mirror entirely covering the back of the bathroom door. Areas of tiling that needed finishing when we were last there in the early summer were now finished. We noticed details such as door handles and window land shutter latches. This was really feeling like finishing touches and I couldn't wait to get out there to see it all and at long last to stay in the house.

Occupation

At last we were making our long-awaited visit to stay in the house. Early April found us flying out with cases loaded with essentials for the house some of which we had been accumulating over the years. The day started with an early flight and a detour from the airport on arrival to shop in Heraklion for towels and bedding. Walking through the busy market in the unaccustomed spring heat after months of winter in Sussex felt strange. It had always been our intention to buy as much for the house as possible on the island. The woman in the bedding shop recalled meeting us and talking about the house the previous year and helped us choose coordinating bedding and towels. Some extras were put in as a house warming gift and we were wished well in our new home. It seemed that the long wait to move in was over at last even though the stay would be more like a camping experience than a stay in a furnished house. We drove down the coast road, through the town and past the shops and harbour. It all seemed reassuringly familiar despite the gap between visits that had stretched to almost a whole twelve months.

We parked behind the church and walked down through the village streets and alleyways in the late afternoon warmth. We unlocked the house and found the bags inside that Manos had been storing for us. Thankfully, we noticed the blow up camping mattress so at least we wouldn't be sleeping on the floor; well we would be but on a mattress. We went around the house opening the shutters and looking at last at the finished house in the flesh. We had seen updates through the winter but often the emailed photos could be as frustrating as they could be informative. What was the texture on the wood? Had the steel been sealed and painted? Would the window be in sunlight in the morning – so many questions and now at last a chance to obtain all the answers for ourselves.

It seemed larger than we had remembered although the lack of furniture helped with this impression. It was also lighter inside. This was the first time we had seen the inside space with the troublesome glass hatch installed and although the glass had an opaque film applied to, at our request, it allowed a large amount of diffused light from the sky into the top room and via the glass floor down into the ground floor room. The glass panels at the back of some of the stair treads were also effective in getting more light into the wet room with the unique multi colour mosaic dramatic tiling. The glass hatch provided us with on of the shocks of the completion. The hi-tech remote control motor installation was probably the most intrusive addition to the ancient building. The architect had resolved the design problem of the hatch by fixing a huge single slab of thick plate glass on the hatch. The weight of this required two electric motor mechanisms to move it; goodness know what it weighed but the motors were supported by an expensive looking black box with a constant bright blue light, an uninterruptible power supply apparently to avoid being stranded on the roof terrace. Operating it provided a trip to the roof terrace with a Thunderbirds or Bond film moment as the motors whirred and whined to raise several hundred pounds of glass slab. Still once it was open the climb up the spiral stairs provided us with a welcome sample what we had first seen in the house, a panoramic view over the red tiled village roofs to the mountains and down to the coast – it was truly one spectacular view. Standing there looking across the olive groves to the roofs of the town, the harbour and the bay, the mountains beyond I recalled some of the frustrations of the project. The time it had taken and the difficulties of communicating from a distance, the cultural differences and the reluctance to admit there were problems or delays. All of that was in the past as was my accident the previous year that almost conspired to end my interest in the house or anything else. Standing together here in the late afternoon sun on our own roof terrace with a fantastic view atop our own little greek house the difficulties fell away – we had done it !!!

Looking around the house seemed larger than we had expected although this was only an impression reinforced by the lack of furniture. This was restricted to a "blow-up" mattress, a folding camping wardrobe upstairs and two flat pack boxes of wall desks.

Downstairs was no less crowded with one large case (bright red) that we had used to bring out essentials, the bench kitchen and our cases. It was too late in the day to organise things today. The evening was the time to be out we would walk into town for sustenance and socialising.

We had arrived early in the season and although the temperature was higher than at home it was colder than usual so donning the warmest coats we had (thin cotton jackets) we walked down to the town. We had planned this in our minds for so long that it was hard to believe we were actually doing it at last. The walk was shorter than we re-membered and in no time at all we were in one of our favourite bars receiving a warm welcome. " How are you? Did you have a good win-ter?" "How is your family? Are you ready for the season?" Then the inevitable question that for so long had required a tactful and opti-mistically evasive answer. "And how is your house – finished yet?" "YES –it is! We moved in today!" Glasses were clinked – the bill was waved and we felt the warmth of cretan friendship wash over us – they were pleased on our behalf. Sure, it meant that we would be more regular customers but there was a genuine feeling that we had joined a community albeit as temporary members still struggling with the in-tricacies of the native language. We announced we were setting off to track down supper and said our goodbyes promising to return. The town seemed very quiet with many of the businesses still opening to shorter winter hours and others not yet open for the season. Behind some of the windows there was evidence of redecorating going on in readiness for the new season. Some of the business owners recognised us and we were ready with our answers for the inevitable questions. "You are back. How is progress with your village house? Is it finished yet?" Our answers brought varying degrees of surprise – and promises of visits now the works had finished – we must get some furniture if we are to entertain. Supper was inside a small brightly painted taverna right next to the blackness of the sea. It was cooked by the owner, we were the only customers and she sat and ate a helping with us while telling us that she used old recipes handed down to her through her family and sourced organically grown ingredients some from her fa-ther's land. The collection of dishes were delicious, small cheese pies, courgette balls and grilled aubergines, oven cooked sliced potato, small meat balls cooked in a spicy tomato gravy and a jug of chilled white wine. Fortified we paid and started the walk home through the town and up the hill to the village, the lights twinkling through the olive groves to spend the first night in our house. The enjoyment of finally living in our own little house in Crete even made the uphill walk home palatable. The next morning I woke up and as often happens on the first morning in a new place wondered where the hell I was. The beams of the ceiling looked unfamiliar the light coming down from above seemed bright but the windows I could see were shuttered. Fi-nally, I realised, I was waking up on the first morning in our house in Crete. Things would seem clearer after a cup of coffee; they always do. The camping mattress had seemed surprisingly comfortable although I think we slept the sleep of the exhausted from a mixture of travel fatigue and excitement. Breakfast was enjoyed on the roof terrace- it was a necessity as there was a wall to sit on and no seats in the house. The view was still breathtaking and there were new sounds as the village woke up to start the day. Chickens were being fed, doors opened and closed, greetings exchanged. Noises of cars and mopeds were more muted as these were mostly parked on the edge of the village with the narrow alleys only accessible to the determined motorist. The bright morning light reflected activity down in the town where cars could be seen moving around and boats shuffling in and out of the harbour. It would be possible to while away many hours just watching and soaking up all of this but things needed to be done. This house needed furniture!

During the lengthy period of the rebuilding of the house there had been plenty of time to consider furniture. This process had included the leisurely browsing of many magazines, visits to furniture shops in Crete and England as well as some exhausting days at design exhibitions in London. The visit to the annual 'Grand Designs' in Docklands seemed particularly ironic for our 2 four metre square rooms; nevertheless the looking had been good fun. Now we were able to 'shop' for real it seemed more daunting. The certainly wasn't room to push any unsuccessful buys into a corner if they didn't work once in the house. We had also decided to shop in Crete even though friends seemed to imagine that we would be hiring a van and driving across Europe and two ferry visits to transport contents bought at home. These were usually people who hadn't seen the range of shops on the island and would not consider themselves driving a van almost 2000 miles!

The wood yard and "coffin making"

Earlier plans for the house had included some cupboard space for clothes, possibly using on of the niches carved out of the thick walls. With the house complete we could see that there wasn't a niche that would readily lend itself to the creation of a wardrobe. As with other matters we were realising that live on the island would be different from home and that clothing tended to be lighter and less bulky as well as less formal. For me shorts or cut offs were with short sleeved shirts or T shirts were day wear and evening wear for most months supplemented by chinos and maybe a light cotton jacket for a cooler evening. Friends on the island had warned us of the likelihood of mice damage to food and clothing particularly in the villages where chickens were popular and the closeness of neighbouring houses and outhouses were 'rodent friendly.' The plans for furnishing the house had always included multipurpose furniture and a storage solution combined with seating seemed to give us certain advantages. We needed seats in the house plus mouse proof storage, so with this in mind I sketched out measurements for some simple hinged lid boxes that would provide just this. Enquiries directed us to a woodyard out of town that look like it was supplying a good proportion of builders on the island judging by the scale of it. We parked the car and I went into he office clutching my piece of paper containing the measurements. i asked at the counter if I could speak English and have some wood cut to size. "Of course" came the friendly answer - "see my son in the building across the yard." The second building was vast with stacks of wood and several large circular saw tables with a man wearing a coating of sawdust over his overalls slicing lengths of wood. He looked up and nodded towards a door in the corner. I knocked and went in to see a younger man, in a collar and tie sitting at a desk. May I speak english I asked. "Of course, what would you like" he answered with a smile putting down the newspaper he was reading which I was surprised to recognise as an edition of the Financial Times, recognisable by it's characteristic pink paper. Clearly my rudimentary greek would not be required.
I showed him the plans for three boxes and explained that i thought ply wood would be best. He agreed and picking up a calculator started punching in numbers. After a minutes he wrote some scribbled numbers on my paper and said "take this over to Iorgos - he will cut it out

of two large pieces of ply. I had some questions -"how much? and when can I collect it?" He looked puzzled - "you don't want to make two journeys - he will cut it now and it will be less than a hundred euros with the cutting. I thanked him and headed towards Iorgos and his cloud of sawdust. He was agreeable to the new task and enrolled me to hold one end of the large wooden sheet as we carried it to the saw table. Removing a pencil from behind his ear and picking up a long metal rule he started marking up the board and once this was done he restarted the large circular saw and muted by the noise he indicated by hand signals we were to feed the sheet towards the spinning blade. Sensibly he positioned himself nearest to the action making sure he got the more lavish coating of sawdust as well as steering the board along the markings. Remarkable, after less than a quarter of an hour the

pieces were all stacked up and he indicated I should drive into the workshop to load up. Outside I was surprised to see my liberal coating of sawdust which was clearly supplied as part of the transaction perhaps as repayment for the unskilled assistance. Once i had paid we set off home, opening all the car windows to let out the freshly cut wood smell and at least some of the sawdust.

At home several hours of assembly followed the next day to produce a set of three strong boxes with hinged lids and thanks to the skilled (and unskilled) cutting the pieces fitted together well with true right angles. The only doubt was the curious looks from some of the neighbours passing at the end of the street seeing me apparently beginning a new village industry of 'coffin making'

Luckily none of them called to commission orders. Once moved into the house and loaded with bedding and our clothes they have proved a secure deterrent against local mice (pondecos) and moths.

Furniture

So some storage had been arranged and the boxes in the kitchen were strong enough to sit on but on the island everyone spent at least some of the time sitting outside and our 'street' or more correctly the alley-way outside was shady from lunchtime onwards. We needed chairs.

The seating upstairs was sorted by ordering some clear perspex small armchairs following the theme of space saving using light; these were found on-line and ordered and collected from a furniture showroom in Heraklion, the capital. The next set of chairs were sourced in a less conventional way.

One morning we had stopped for a cold drink of frappe in one of the restaurants beside the sea towards the causeway and we were chatting with the owner as he set out the tables and chairs for the days business. "Have you moved into your house yet ?" upon hearing that we had we were pleasantly surprised to be asked if we needed any chairs. Gosh, yes thanks we need some -"How many? I am clearing out a relatives restaurant I have a load of old, traditional style wicker seated chairs, the type used in all the old places but not used nowadays."

We agreed on pair even though Dimitris said he had dozens to get rid of. "I don't want anything for them, you are good customers, I will drop them up at your house in the village - i will find it I have seen the photos. Good as his word later that week we found two chairs left outside our house and they were splendid, cane seats and carved backs, one with a bird motif the other a horned kri-kri a cretan goat/deer creature - wonderful!

The following week after agonising whether we were cheeky enough to request another two from Dimitri's surplus hoard we were driving through the municipal dump in one of the nearby villages when we spotted two traditional chairs placed next to the large, green wheeled bins. We knew this was the local method of recycling - rubbish thrown in the bins, anything still serviceable and oaf possible use to someone else was placed near the bins. W made our getaway - so a set of four similar traditional dining chairs - cost nil ! Though we would need to be sure to keep our custom up at Dimitri's restaurant, this would not be a hardship.

The most pressing item of furniture we needed was the sofa bed. We had been sleeping on a blow up mattress for the first week or so made easier by a dedicated electric pump but it still need reflating each night. It was surprisingly comfortable but not a long term solution. Unfortunately the first few furniture shops we had tried had drawn a blank with sofa beds that were either cheap foam or larger sofas that would never fit. It did seem to be a feature of many of the newer, large furniture out of
town emporiums that they were catering for large apartments or villas judging by the scale of their pieces, and their prices. Not quite at the point of desperation we were driving south to Ierapetra known as the home town of the island's 'fruit millionaires' rich from their proceeds from the huge areas of poly tunnels covering large parts of the plains and hills in the south. Just before entering the town we spotted a small furniture showroom at the side of the road with small chairs and sofas on display. We parked and went in asking if any of these sofas converted to double beds. Th usual cretan reply of "Of course- let me show you" After both of us trying both sofa and bed mode for comfort we were ready to buy. 'Can you deliver?'
'Of course. What is your address?'
'We are in a village with no street name or number'

'No matter give us your phone number and we will phone when near-by.'

After agreeing a price for the display one to be delivered the next morning - discounted ! we paid and left our number.

The next morning I sat on the roof with a cup of coffee, mobile and sun hat and glasses. We had a bird's eye view of the road up to the village from the coast - assuming that would be the most obvious route. I needn't have worried as my phone rang -"we are driving up to the village from the coast now." I scanned the road for the delivery van - until I saw our new purchase on the back of an old pick up, roped down, the front resting on the cab roof.

' I can see you - I will meet you bey the church where the cars are parked'

On hearing the house was some two or three hundred metres away the delivery men decided they would drive through the narrow village streets - I ran ahead only just able to stop them driving the last fifty yards - down the steps! Between them the two guys carried the sofa to the front door where it was quickly established even with the cushions removed it was not going to go through the front door. It didn't look like it would easily dismantle but one of them spotted the small double doors upstairs where we planning a small balcony . A quick

measuring established that it would fit if we could get it up there. A pause for cold drinks and contemplation led to the suggestion from the larger of the deliverers that they would push it up to the doors to me and two of us would hold it - one from below, onc above while the smaller and presum-ably faster delivery man would run upstairs and together we would manhandle it inside, It sounded unlikely but worth a try. To my surprise it succeeded, no-one was injured and we had a bed

The photo search

This particular episode in our life illustrates the strange forces of co-incidence that seem to centre on the island. One winter evening in greek school at home in Sussex, Christina, one of our class members handed us a large A3 black and white photo. It showed a typical small cretan fishing boat complete with a cretan fisherman moored close to the shore with the corner of a stone building in the background. "My husband took this when we were staying on Crete in the 1970's – he thinks it's your village." We thanked her for the photo and took it home. Later this year when sorting stuff out in the house the photo resurfaced and we thought we should bring it with us to the island to see if we could identify the location or the fisherman although this seemed quite unlikely after all this time. A few days into the stay we remembered to take the photo into town with us and try to tie down the location. We didn't know whether the places that were used for moorings had changed over time but there were a couple of likely places where stone buildings were near the shore. A brief discussion in the first café suggested the road towards the causeway by the old carob factory. We knew this location as it had recently been opened as a lovely restaurant that quickly had become one of our favourites to eat at. When we arrived there Dimitri, one of the co-owners, became very excited and took the photo over to the edge of the building that abutted onto his restaurant and pointed out to us that the wall shown in the was the same as in the photo. He asked if he could borrow it and copy or scan it to display on the wall of the restaurant. We readily agreed and said we would collect the original the following week but asked him if he knew or could find out who the person was in the pho-to. A few days later Dimitri called to us as we were walking past and returned the photo but admitted he had not been able to find out the identity of the mystery fisherman perhaps he was no longer in the town or even no longer alive. It was hard to exactly put on age on the fisherman – he appeared to have a good head of black curls and was probably between mid-twenties and his thirties. So if the photo was taken in 1975 then we were looking for a 60 to 70 year old.
We walked back to the town square and settled down to an iced coffee in our favourite bar. The owner was a local "lad" like so many in the town but probably too young to recognise the mystery fisherman but

when we told him the story he quickly entered into the spirit of the quest. "I don't readily recognise him but my father might. We'll ask him shortly when he calls by." When his father arrived there was a close scrutiny of the photo with the necessary swapping of reading glasses from distance ones. " It could be George! He normally walks this way most mornings." In a moment of pure coincidence George was spotted on the other side of the road carrying his shopping walking next to the harbour. Nectarios ran towards him carrying the photo followed at a more sedate pace by his Dad. As he approached the "suspect" he slowed and after a short conversation over the photo they returned to the bar – "No, it's not him but there is a Manolis who is the right age and had curly hair – maybe we should ask in the cafenion." This was a good suggestion but a little intimidating as the most popular cafenion in town was certainly full of potential "suspects" on a daily basis. Although we used the cafenions in the village the two in town had always looked "too Cretan" and full of local men smoking, playing backgammon and drinking their thick black greek coffees and rakis. Also conversation was conducted at high speed and volume with gesticulation bordering on violence. It was still rare to see obvious non-greeks in there though I am sure we would be made welcome. The idea of trying to identify a stranger from some 30 plus years ago with the help of 20 plus cretan pensioners fuelled on nicotine, strong alcohol and caffeine was not an immediately attractive prospect. Wisdom suggested we would defer the task for another day. A few days later our curiousity again got the better of us and we tried another approach. The shop next to the most popular cafenion is owned and run by a couple that we have chatted with over all the years we had visited the town. Their English was far superior to our greek and we wondered if George would be a good interpreter to attempt the extension of the search to the cafenion. After exchanging the usual pleasantries and enquiring about families, business and progress on our house completion I produced the photo. After a short scrutiny there was a feeling that he was familiar; Eleni suggested that her mother may have a better idea so she was summoned from her chair outside for her opinion. This suggestion provided something of a breakthrough. Eleni's Mum took one look at the photo, laughed and said Michaelis Mathiakis – and something else which George translated for us –"she says it's not a recent photo!" So was he still alive, still in the town, where? It was suggested that he lived somewhere off the main road south out of the

town – opposite the causeway road and in a house somewhere behind the restaurant with a pizza oven. Pretty specific directions then – we would follow them up before any other theories on identity were offered.

That afternoon we drove to the south end of town, parked by the nearest restaurant opposite the causeway junction and went inside looking for a pizza oven. Once we established with one of the three staff who appeared to be decorating the restaurant that we were not actually in the market for a mid-afternoon pizza but looking for someone the now familiar photo scrutiny ritual began. After a few moments the trio broke into laughter eventually explaining that yes it was Michaelis, he lived nearby the last house up the hill at the side of the restaurant – no need to drive – it is nearby. Again the comment was added – it is not a recent picture – followed by more laughter. We walked up the hill and around two corners and came to a large two storey traditional style house with a large wrap around balcony and blue shutters behind a metal gate and high railings. This must be it so we opened the gate and walked through a beautiful garden full of vegetables, flowers and fruit trees. We rang the door bell and waited but there was no answer. Some brick steps led around the side and upstairs to another door with a bell but again there was no response. Disappointed we left – was it the right house? As we came out a woman walked by who we recognised as someone who led here sheep past Marias apartment when we used to stay there. They were taking to graze up on the hillside and brought back in the evening. We asked if this was the house of Michaelis Mathiakis – 'yes, of course." We planned to return and try again.

It took two more visits before the evening that the door was answered by a man with a smiling but puzzled face and receding curly grey hair. The brief conversation was curtailed by Michaelis laughing out loud at the image of a very much younger self in the photo. His wife was called and introductions made with some confusion caused by our (very) halting greek and their virtual non-existent English. Nevertheless, we were ushered within "please, sit down – what would you like to drink?" We settled on orange juice, partly because we knew the word for it in greek but also because clear heads would be needed for the conversation. The house was large and cool with a polished marble floor and comfortable furnishings in the typical greek style. We explained that a friend in England had given us the picture and we believed it was taken over 30 years ago in Elounda. He pointed out the window the part of the coast where the photo was taken – it was the building next to the old carob factory – and we think he said that he still had the boat. The conversation was interrupted by Mrs Mathiakis who was stocking up the coffee table with mezedas, in between laughing again at the photo. These included chopped cucumber, olives, dakos with tomatoes and pepper and it wasn't long before the inevitable carafe of raki and a tray of small shots glasses appeared, (so much for keeping a clear head.) The conversation slowly arrived at where we lived and after a diversion to England we explained about the small holiday home in the village above the town. "I have a house there as well" explained a surprised Michaelis, "where is yours?" This part always proved difficult as we had to give directions to a house without a number or name in the street with no name. We gave our normal description of the turning between the two cafenions and down - more surprise – "mine is also there!" much laughter – we appeared to be neighbours!

Conversation continued in a combination of our halting greek and hand signals supplemented by photos on my ipod – all time Michaelis and his wife both of whom had beautiful open faces with ready smiles. The usual questions that are quickly asked in Crete to the surprise of more reserved northern Europeans –"How old are you, do you have children, how old – what do you do?" This revealed that Michaelis was 65 and he reckoned he was 30 when the photo was taken. Eventually, our greek vocubulary exhausted and our stomachs full we attempted to leave. "You must come up to see our house in the village." We believed the reply was positive but were surprised to hear that they would visit in one hours time. We must leave and prepare some food to welcome them and tidy up! This was easier said than done – Eleni disappeared into the kitchen and quickly re-emerged carrying two bags. One was full of fresh lemons from the garden the other full of large brown eggs. After leaving the house we made the mistake of admiring the flowers in the garden, our leaving was interrupted by the cutting of a huge bunch of flowers to take. They were pink and white amaryllis, the sort that are grown at home one at a time indoors in a pot at Christmas; here they filled a flower border. As we left through the gate laden with gifts and saying our goodbyes a young man got out of his car and walked towards the gate. Michaelis called his over and introduced him as their nephew who turned out to be a civil engineer working at one of the large new hotel developments just up the coast. To our relief he spoke perfect English and understood about the photo and his uncle coming to see us – he also corrected our understanding of the return visit – it was tomorrow at 9 o'clock not tonight – so much for our greek – what else had we got wrong?

The next morning we were up early and tidied the little house after our breakfast on the roof terrace. The flowers were in our largest jug – we had yet to acquire a flower vase and we were ready to receive a visit from our new friends. They were on time and were also not empty handed carrying a large bottle of olive oil – their own pressing so we believed. There was more laughter and pointing by Michaelis to the other side of the street across the two metre wide alleyway. Eventually, the penny dropped, the house opposite was his. While the building work went on the architect had arranged the use of a store room for building materials in the house opposite, a sort of basement room. It wasn't clear to us where the front door of the house was and whether it was part of the occupied house that backed onto it. We knew that house lived in by yet another Maria. Some time ago we had asked the architect whether it was possible for us to continue to use this room which seemed separate from any other house. It would be useful for storage which given the size of our house would be a great help. It appeared that through a distant coincidence we had blundered upon the owner ourselves …. And he was our new friend! Coffee and orange juice was offered round along with biscuits and we showed our new friends around the house. The bathroom tiling and the glass floor caused the usual surprise but all in all the house was judged as "oriel" or beautiful. The view from the roof terrace with the panoramic distant views was enthused over and we tried to explain that this had provided the design stimulus for the house with the need for access coupled with the requirement to get light down into the house.

Having shown them around our house it was indicated that we should look around the house opposite so finishing our drinks we followed Michaelis around the corner where he climbed the small set of stone steps and producing a key, unlocked the door into the upstairs of the house opposite.

The house was still furnished though the cobwebs suggested any occupation was not recent. There were a series of upstairs rooms leading one from the other, four in all with a window that was blocked in the third one that would face our house. The last one, the kitchen had a window towards the sea and a door onto the small balcony. The furniture was the traditional cretan style, including a table cloth still on the table! The second room had a round brick wall in it that was apparently a well! It was an education and strange to think that our own house was the other side of the wall across the narrow street. Our greek vocabulary didn't allow extensive discussion of interior design details so after hopefully showing the right amount of polite enthusiasm we all came back out into our street but the house viewing was not yet over. Eleni led us back up the street towards the church and after exchanging greetings with Zambia outside her cafenion and , I think, a promise to return, she directed us up a set of stone stairs and unlocked a first story door. We believe she said this had been a house that used to belong to her aunt but wresting with verb tenses was proving one of the greater grammatical challenges of the greek language. She opened up and we went in. It was a large room and once she opened the shutters we could see a table and chairs, a 50's style kitchen unit, several large trunks and a full sized loom! The electricity was still connected and she said it was for sale – but before we got into negotiations, or worse any commitment to buy, we quickly explained that one Crete house was plenty for us, (there had been moment in the previous years when that had seemed a surplus!) S. was particularly taken by the contents of the trunks which had been opened to show rolls of fabric and pieces of embroidery. This was the second house in the village that had been found to have a loom in – perhaps this was typical or were we in some textile centre of the island? We were also shown downstairs and a throwaway remark was made that seemed to suggest the ownership of several other village houses. We suggested beating a retreat back to the safety of the cafenion but concluded that the sales patter was very low key and almost incidental. We also were selfishly thinking of a way to bring up the subject of the store room opposite but felt that it wasn't the right time and concluded it should be left until a later visit as currently we only had the pithori, one old wooden box and a few old wooden shutters that needed storing and thought we would probably leave them out in the alley until our next visit.

A few days into the next visit we were walking out from the house to the hire car to drive out for the day when we were called with a cheery "kalimera!" – it was Michaelis and Eleni getting out of their car near the church. We explained in our best greek that we were back again for a few weeks and agreed that we would meet again – "come to my house again when you are next in town" – we agreed that we would with some slight trepidation at the thought of trying to discuss renting the store room and wondering if our phrase book or dictionary covered the correct terms for "storage" and "old junk" and other useful terms. Later that same week after a few hours wrestling with a greek dictionary and a phrase book S. announced that she had prepared a letter, in greek, to explain our request to rent this small room – having discovered the greek word for a store room – "an apothiki." Fortified with this new information and bearing gifts of wine and biscuits we paid an early evening call on Michaelis and Eleni. The welcome was warm and chairs and a table were pulled out onto their large balcony where as the sun set we engaged in mutual misunderstandings in greek and broken English. Less naïve friends had already instructed us in the art of greek negotiating and we had been given clear advice on not settling on the first price offered and to be tenacious including the need for essential hand and head gestures. Of course, these became less clear once the wine had been opened and poured along with the inevitable raki and a veritable feast of mezedas.

Michaelis was invited to read the letter which he did accompanied by some smiles and chuckles. We awaited the response while we tried to summon up the greek negotiating secrets that had been supplied to us earlier. They proved completely unnecessary, if we understood Michaelis correctly he was saying we must just use the space, for free ! We were friends and no rent was expected. This was very generous and completely undermined our negotiating strategy. Our only concern was whether we had completely misinterpreted the response but concluded that this would have to be cleared up another time as the wine and the raki were already conspiring to make "clearing any-thing up" a bit tricky. After several hours our greek and drinking ca-pacity exhausted we made our goodbyes and headed for home but not before a date was made for morning coffee in the village cafenion the following Sunday morning. Perhaps this would be an opportunity to confirm our storage arrangements- who knows. We walked off towards our house not entirely clear whether we were greek shed owners or not – things were never straightforward or predictable here – maybe that's what we liked? We decided to avoid moving any items into the neighbouring stone "shed" until the arrangements were positively con-firmed and hoped to do that on Sunday, over coffee.

When Sunday came we made our way up into the centre of the village which is only two minutes from our house. There seemed a hub-bub of conversation coming from inside Zambia's cafenion so we went inside. The single room was packed and as our eyes adjusted to the more subdued light compared with the bright sun outside we were hailed across the room, "Geoff, Stephania!- Pame" It was Michaelis and as we squeezed across the room towards him others there greeted us- "kalimera, kalimera" It seemed that knowing Michaelis was an instant popularity ticket. Zambia came over in a newly laundered pinafore and took our orders – a coffee and a juice – cheeks were kissed, hands shaken and shoulders patted. Biscuits and cakes were offered by Michaelis as we squeezed onto the table next to him – introductions were made but we had arrived in the middle of a number of quickfire greek conversations – and they were far to rapid and complex for us to follow so we just sat and enjoyed the hospitality, drank our drinks and ate our biscuits and smiled, probably idiotically, at anyone who looked at us. Occasionally, we heard Michaelis mention in greek, Maria's house and the word for English and new friends but mostly the talk was more somber and as people slowly left they came and shook Michaelis's hand. Shortly afterwards Michaelis rose and pulled some notes out of his pocket and handed them to Zambia then he said good bye to us. The words "apothiki" and OK were used again but we had still failed to confirm the arrangements completely to our satisfaction. Another time perhaps and later we understood a little more as the same afternoon, on one of the obituary notices posted at points around the town, we noticed the name of "Mathiakis" – did this mean that Michaelis was marking the funeral or anniversary of a relative when entertaining people to food and drink at the cafenion. We felt guilty that we had not understood the situation so that we could at least pass on our condolences.

In the village a day or two later we thought of a new tactic. One of our neighbours, a Belgian lady, Katerina was something of a linguist speaking enough greek to work in one of the hotels. Over a conversation in the cafenion we explained our dilemma and how we wanted to be certain that the arrangements were alright before we started moving stuff into the room. It transpired that she already knew Michaelis from the church and the cafenion – it was agreed, she would ring him up on our behalf. That same evening we were walking down to town through the olive groves and stopped to admire an old net at the side of the path all bundled up but complete with the little cork floats that we had started collecting when we found them washed up on the beach. I was just lamenting the fact that my pocket knife was not with me when we were hailed in greek by a woman's voice. A woman wearing an apron emerged from a gateway in the stone wall bordering the olive trees. To our surprise it was Eleni, Michaelis's wife. Our pleasure at seeing her again was tempered by the memory that she spoke no English at all and that our attempts at limited greek conversation had convinced her, on past experience, that we could understand her greek especially if she spoke to us at 80 miles per hour. Once we had got beyond good evening and established that all of us and the absent Michaelis were well and that the weather was still good we were lost. Whatever she was saying was completely lost on us – was she relaying the content of a discussion that had taken place with Katerina ? Who knows – we shrugged and apologised and tried to leave but she became more agitated and gestured at the land beyond the walls under the trees and spoke more rapid, dense and sadly unintelligible(to us) greek; reminding us again how much work was needed on our language classes. We finally said our goodbyes and beat a retreat into town for a welcome evening drink.

The next development was when Katerina called to say that she had spoken to Michaelis and as we had first thought he was happy to let us use the apothiki for free. We thanked her and mentioned that we had encountered Eleni and not understood what she had said. "Well you may have a chance to clear this up as Michaelis has suggested that you call round to their house in town one afternoon or evening as he is worried." "What about?" we asked a little anxiously. Apparently he had expressed concern to Katerina that our belongings may suffer damage from damp or mice if left in the store and he would like us to use the empty house upstairs and would give us a key for us to use it as a safer and more secure store. This presented us with something of a dilemma as we wanted to store some old shutters and original wood from before the building works as well as some outside chairs (recent "rescued" from the municipal tip.) We had been concerned that we would be re-introducing rot or wood worm back into the house and damage the new timber in it but we certainly weren't planning to damage Michaelis's house. The subject would delicate discussion.

Later that week we were due to leave the island to return to England. We knew we must meet Michaelis and Eleni before we left and before we placed or "treasures" in the storeroom – or infested his house with them. We couldn't delay any longer so we found ourselves early on evening climbing the hill to his house and walking through his well-stocked garden. There was no need to knock as Michaelis was sitting on his veranda reading the paper –"kalimera- hello my friends!" – we joined him and admired the view of the bay glimpsed through some gaps in the neighbouring houses. We smiled at each other and exchanged embraces and Eleni disappeared into the house as we sat down and braced ourselves for a greek language workout. We had come prepared having researched with a dictionary and phrase book a prepared statement. It was along the lines of –"we thank you for your kind offer of the use of your house for our possessions but they will only be old things and items such as paint and ladders and outside furniture etc that we have no room for in our small house. Are you sure you do not want to be paid any rent?" We skirted around the fact that we were worried about introducing greek woodworm into either of our houses and felt that this would not be an issue in the storeroom as we had already noticed and abundance of existing woodworm and mice droppings there. Michaelis laughed and as far as we could tell after putting on his reading glasses and examining the note carefully he seemed to confirm it was ok to use the apothiki as we were his new friends – now we eat! Eleni reappeared and introduced a range of delicious mezedas – salads, tomato and garlic paste on rusks, calamari, hard cheeses and boiled eggs. This was accompanied by raki for Michaelis and me and more gentile wine for the ladies. We sat eating smiling at one another and admiring the garden and the evening view of the bay and the mountains across the rooftops. Suddenly, Eleni became very vocal and said something that made Michaelis laugh we didn't understand any of it apart from what sounded like the work for eggs. Slowly, Michaelis asked whether we liked eggs. As we had already eaten some in the mezedas we confirmed that we did and said that these were very good. He explained they were their eggs from the garden in the hills and he and Eleni laughed again. After several wrong turns we eventually understood that the earlier encounter with Eleni was when she was up at the small-holding feeding the chickens and we had (unbeknown to us) refused her offer of some eggs. We could only apologise, both for our rude rebuttal to her kindness and for our poor greek. Michaelis explained it was of no consequence and all was ok now. So we were now not only home owners but also enjoyed storage rights in a greek "shed" – life was good.

Lepers

Until we visited Crete I had only really heard about lepers in stories in the bible. Near our village was the site of a greek leper colony that had existed on a separate island previously a venetian fort and within sight of the coast. It was a popular tourist attraction with boat trips arranged from the nearby harbours along the coast. Recent years had seen the publication of a fictionalised account of life on the island in the 1930's to 50's by an English writer Victoria Hislop. The book had become an international best seller and was being serialised by a greek TV company in a multi million euro production. Filming was taking place in actual locations and specially created sets in and around the island.

The year we moved into the house there was some filming in the village using the village streets as a proxy for the leper colony on the island. The narrow streets and style of houses was similar to those on the island itself. As much of the filming took place under lights at night it was rather strange to leave the restaurants and bars at the coast as they were winding down for the night to find film production in full swing under lights, often until 2 or 3 a.m. There were also some minor starring roles for the elderly ladies in the village which they were delighted with although they complained that the dust and red earth that had been put down to cover the more modern paved street was getting into their houses.

Our next encounter with the film crew was to launch us on a belated quest for film stardom. We were eating a late supper in one of the restaurants in town when we spotted a lot of bright lights across the bay at the causeway. On asking what was going on we were told that

the Canal Bar was being used for filming that evening and the previous night it had gone on late into the night. We agreed to stroll over there and see what could be seen. On arrival we could see the usual maze of wires and lights, monitors and consoles behind the collection of film crew vans and cars. In a break in filming we walked nearer to the restaurant to get a clearer look when much to our surprise one of the smartly suited actors shyly waved at us. "Is that Stelios" - it certainly looked like him. He got up and came over – 'Kalinithka - how are you ?" he said sheepishly. "what are you doing?" – he laughed –"I'm an extra and this is my second night eating and drinking at the film company's expense" – before he could say much more the cast was called to be quiet for a take.

We watched for around half an hour more and waving goodnight to Stelios went off to bed –it was almost two a.m after all.

The next day in his gallery we spotted a bleary eyed Stelios –'what time did you finish?" –"Not sure he muttered- too much raki"

I thought actors drank water or cold tea – not so in Crete apparently! We said what an interesting experience it must have been and he agreed, then asked us if we wanted to appear as extras. Laughing we said we were due to go back to Sussex the following week and proba- bly wouldn't have time –though eating and drinking in a restaurant at someone else's expense wasn't something I had much opportunity to do since retiring. Stelios said that the casting director was calling into his shop regularly when in town to use his wifi connection – he would see if he could get us parts. Non speaking eating and drinking parts were my preference.

The next day my phone rang and it was Stelios asking us to call by his shop if we were nearby as Zoe was in there and was looking for extras. Some twenty minutes later having met her and shaken hands we were asked to report on Monday morning at 10.30 outside the old school in one of the nearby villages for our film debuts. I reflected that some people work a lot harder on their first auditions. In a fit of conscience I asked whether Stelios had mentioned our imminent return to England and we would only be available for two days. That was fine and could be accommodated – 'just bring yourselves – costumes, make up and lunch would be provided' and bring your greek bank account details to receive payment. We were a bit stunned this seemed a swift selection process but as the house needed to be closed up for the winter and we had to pack and say good-byes to people we put the filming out of our minds until the Monday.

The Sunday of that weekend we had been told that there was to be a premiere of the series to be shown on a large screen in the nearest large town. Given our future opportunity for stardom later that week we felt we should go along and view this. There were no posters around so we had to rely on local rumour to establish the timing of this cultural event – opinions varied between 8 p.m. and 10 p.m. but given the Greeks reputation as night owls I felt a 9 o'clock arrival to be a safe bet. I should have realised how popular the event was to prove when normal on street parking in the usual places proved difficult. After eventually squeezing into a space and parallel parking more or less in line with the pavement and in stark contrast to most of the cars in the street who resembled abandoned get away cars we made our way to the venue in the town square next to the lake. As we wound our way through the backstreets we could hear a hubbub of voices and entering the square we were amazed to see it was packed with a crowd of thousands of people. I led us to a vantage point next to a tree near the back of the crown but the size of the screen suggested we would have a reasonable view. I sent a couple of texts to friends who I thought might be there as well although our chances of pushing through the crowd to one another may not be easy. After a while what looked like a trailer for the series started up on the big screen accompanied by atmospheric music. The crowd settled down as a group of people came onto the stage to generous applause from the enthusiastic crowd. The first speech was from a grey haired gent which was , naturally, in greek at the end of which two small children came on stage to much applause carrying two bouquets of flowers as big as themselves. These were presented to a small dark haired lady in a white dress that we recognised as Victoria the author of the book. She gave a ten minute speech, in what sounded to us to be very good greek and was rewarded with rapturous applause from the crowd. The screen lit up again and the first episode of the series was screened. Frankly, having watched continental European television over the years my expectations were not terribly high but I was quickly proved mistaken. The filming was beautiful, the scenery, the acting, the lighting and the use of music could not have been improved upon – it truly was a revelation. The screening was only briefly marred by a heavy rain shower near the end of the episode when the crowd rather than running for cover picked up the white plastic chairs they had been sitting on and held them upside down over their heads. We were fortunate to be underneath a leafy tree for shelter. The rain only lasted a few minutes and the screening closed to more rapturous and well deserved applause. We left for a late supper and a sobering drink nearer home - we had a busy day tomorrow, our film careers were to start and the standards of the first episode were high.

When the day of filming arrived we drove up to the village following the directions we had been given and found the film company's vans and cars parked outside the village school. We parked the hire car and spotted Zoe carrying a clip-board. She welcomed us and ticked off our names before directing us through a gateway opposite the school. The film crew had taken over the garage and basement storeroom of a house to serve as the make-up studio and wardrobe rooms. We smiled at three or four other "extras" sitting on chairs and tentatively asked what happens next. They had been told to wait for our wardrobe fittings before going into make-up so we joined them on the chairs. One by one we were called into the back of the building where several racks of clothes were hanging. The ladies had been directed towards a selection of "grannie" style skirt and cardigan ensembles which appeared to be woollen. Given that the previous day's temperature had peaked in the low thirties and today felt no cooler this seemed unfortunate. For me there was worse to come, the men were directed to woolly "long john" style combinations that reminded me of George Clooney's outfit as an escaped prisoner in "Oh Brother, where Art thou." After several attempts to find a set that would at least allow me to sit down and breathe I was relieved that a set in thick cotton rather than wool was produced and these were marginally more comfortable. The young woman in charge of the costumes was initially rather cool towards us but I think the effort of overfed western Europeans trying to squeeze into the costumes cheered her up and she was more good natured at the end than the beginning of the fitting, even sewing up my waistband without injuring me. Trooping back outside we were all told to await our make up. The make up team comprised one woman and two darkly dressed guys with exotic hairstyles and facial hair who turned out to be a pair of greek brothers from Melbourne who were top international make-up artists having worked on Harry Potter as well as other big productions.

Their English/Australian was excellent as they effortlessly switched between talking english to the extras and greek to the main actors.

Their excellent English and good humour allowed us to find out a little more about the day. It appeared that we would be all made up either as patients or visitors in the leprosy hospital. Those that were patients would have facial make up applied to simulate leprosy and this would be quite time consuming with filming of our scenes not anticipated until after lunch but once we were made up we could help ourselves to drinks and snacks over in the school car park. Never having suffered leprosy before I wasn't sure how long the make up would take so when they offered a seat I readily volunteered. Now perhaps I had been daydreaming after the George Clooney wardrobe offerings but I thought that after a whole hour in make up that I would be looking pretty damn good for my big screen debut. I must have forgotten that 'leper' was the operative word here. Most of my time in make up was spent constructing a large buboe on my chin and the side of my face. This was build up with some kind of rubber solution that brought back the nostalgic smells of youthful Airfix model kits. The paint was applied over the top and allowed to dry. It felt strange and looked horrific! S. was given a similar "growth" but hers also was above her mouth. When we finished laughing –(with care) the effect became strangely moving and realised how families must have seen their loved ones disfigured by the dreadful disease. The look was topped off by a visit from "the dirty girl" – not what you might think, she seemed quite refined but put grease in our hair and dirtied our knuckles and fingernails! This had all taken quite a while so the offer of a coffee or a cold

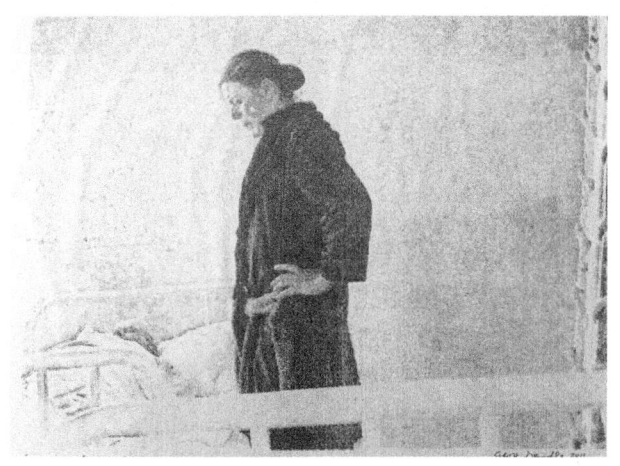

drink was very welcome and having collected we sat in the shade under a tree with our fellow lepers. After a while with only a couple of the extras having been called onto the set inside the school we were told it was time for lunch. A number of local business vans had arrived earlier and laid out an appetising spread of food under a canopy in the corner of the playground. We were also warned to eat carefully and afterwards return to the make up area to be "touched up." The day showed promise!

Eating was more difficult than I anticipated as one side of my face felt heavier than the other at gave me a lop-sided feeling. The warning was timely as I could feel water i.e. 'sweat' had broken out under the prosthetic and was running down my neck. After a delicious and welcome lunch we returned to the make-up team for our 'repairs'. These were swiftly executed and we were called back to the school this time for me to go onto the set and lie down on one of the beds. This was welcome as the school room seemed much hotter than the shade in the playground. Still it seemed mine was not to be an action role – I was tempted to practice my groaning but felt I had better wait for direction as there was already a lot of shouting and gesticulating in greek to the actors with more demanding roles. Best to enjoy the lie down and digest my lunch. The scene seemed to consist of a consultation between the two doctors at the bed of one patient while I was one of three other patients lying in adjacent beds. It was a revelation seeing the scene with the doctors; one had arrived for make-up when we were in there and in a matter of minutes had been transformed from a cool, fashionable 20-something to a middle-aged world-weary, middle-aged professional with high waisted trousers, greying hair and lined face and even an older walk. The issue of walking was to cause me trouble later in the filming. We were not directed to groan and after several takes we were directed outside to the relative cool of the playground.

The other extras were interested in what was happening inside and eagerly quizzed us for indications of when they would be required for their own big screen appearances. We didn't have long to wait. After welcome cold drinks all the extras were directed into the hospital ward were we were assigned roles as patients or visitors. There was to be a busy scene shot of the whole room with the doctors and nurses, visitors and treatment for the patients. Cameras on trolleys were wheeled in and lighting was adjusted – there were even clapper boards used with shouts of one, two, three, four, - Go shouted. Our roles today were mainly limited to lying on the beds looking leprous – not to taxing although the room was still warm and stuffy made worse by most of the greeks smoking enthusiastically during any break in actual filming. There was one distraction when I was directed to do a "walk off" part across the ward and up the corridor. This was rather ironic as I had mentioned in make up (how easily we drifted into 'thesp. speak") that my single previous venture onto screen had been in a corporate video where I had been quite happy talking on camera but when asked to end the piece by casually walking across the office had botched several takes, in the eyes of the director, by 'unnatural walking'? Eventually the piece ended with me sitting after several abortive takes. So walking on camera may not be a natural skill for me.

Anyway, when 'action' or more correctly "Pame !" in greek was called I hitched up my itchy hospital pyjamas and made my way across the ward and up the corridor in a manner that I thought would be appropriate to a leper.... A second take was called ..... and a third until I was taken to one side by the assistant director and by her that I walked more like a cowboy than a leper – I think the scene was left on the cutting room floor as I didn't see it when we eventually watched episode 15 some months later.

I recalled that when we had volunteered ourselves for this experience there was talk of "a few hours" – possibly from 11 to 3 or 4 o'clock. It was now past 7 o'clock and the same complex take seemed to be showing no sign of being finalised. The day had proved to be most entertaining and we had chatted with other members of the cast and crew, both greeks and foreign extras. Lunch had been very democratic with everyone helping themselves to meat and salad dishes and all sitting in the playground on chairs or handy walls in the shade. The director was quietly spoken but had great authority and was clearly respected by the cast and crew. He was supported by a more vocal

"The Island" Clouds ⅔₀   Geoff Dandle 2010

blonde female assistant director who marshalled everyone for each
take and who's word on the set seemed to be law. The English author
was also present on the set for part of the day and was very happy to
chat with everyone and expressed her delight in the good reception
the premier had been received the previous evening. We were told
that they had all been working together for almost a whole year and
the whole group had obviously developed a real understanding and
affection for one another. The room had cooled down as the light outside faded and it was with some relief that we were told at 8.30 that
filming for the day had finished –our 'buboes' and costumes had to be
returned to the make up and costume rooms and we were reminded to
return the next day by 10 in the morning.

For us it was a rush home to shower and eat before going to a bar in
town where we had been promised seats for the showing on Greek tv
of the first episode of the series.

When we arrived Nectarios had arranged seats in front of a large tv
screen in the corner of the bar where we were the only members of
the audience – the rest of the customers were facing the other way
watching some euro football event. Armed with drinks we settled down
to enjoy the first episode for the second time. Just after it started another couple joined us and asked us if we knew what it was all about.

We told them of the reception given to the premier on the previous evening and we agreed that the production values looked very high for a tv series. Modesty prevented us from revealing our newfound stardom – we would see how the second day of filming before facing the press and our public.

Day two found us arriving early and taking our places in the costume room where our names had been pinned to yesterday's outfits. We then took our turns in make up with the make up experts checking the photos that had been taken of us previously to ensure continuity. Our face buboes had been preserved in cling film in a cool-box and these were refixed and carefully matched in to the rest of our make up. A visit from our new old friend "the dirty girl" and we were ready to be called onto the set. There was less "hanging about" for me as I was called in for some more lying down action on the periphery of another hospital scene. The rest of the morning was spent drinking coffee and cold drinks under the shade of the trees in the playground. I have neglected to mention the most horrific part of the filming. In amongst the death bed scenes and horrendous disfigurements the issue causing the most disgust and comment among crew and cast, greek and foreigners had been ....the Turkish Toilet!!

This was in the far corner of the playground and provided the only available sanitation. In fact it had been cited as the main reason for many of the crew to volunteer to "nip to town" to get some tape, cups, batteries – in fact anything and use the 21 st century plumbing facilities that were so readily available now on the rest of the island.

The following year a friend of a friend mentioned her part as an extra and within seconds said "And the Turkish toilet – Gross!!"

We were told that an early lunch would be called then we would all be required in the hospital ward for a key scene. Lunch was eaten and the Turkish facilities braved before we reassembled in the ward. There was a delay while post lunch adjustments were made to the make up and checks were made on costumes. S. received a reprimand from the continuity lady for removing her cardigan an essential fashion item in the 30 plus degrees and all was ready. The first part of the shooting was another deathbed scene with the set crowded with visitors and at least one priest. Each 'patient' had a visitor on their bed and they were told to look concerned while the patients were told to look 'sickly' – conjuring up the memory of the Turkish facilities certainly helped me with this although it would probably be best not to actually be sick over our visitor as we had barely been introduced and mine was now holding hands with me! The action centred on the bed opposite and much wailing and crying was accompanied by chanting from the priest until eventually the sheet was pulled over he head of the 'deceased' and there followed discussion between the director and the camera crew as to whether the 'corpse' could be seen to be still breathing under the sheet. He was told to hold his breathe for the latter part of the subsequent take. After a few more takes and everyone needing a short break from the crying and chanting the filming moved to a neighbouring bed where one of our British extras was advised he would be next to 'act dead.' I was secretly relieved that he had been chosen over me given the criticism I had already received for my walking and had concluded that a convincing 'dying' may not be within my dramatic range. One of the things that was impressive to us as thespian newcomers was the way the professional actors assumed their screen personas on demand. The two doctors were a pair of young comedians clowning around together and teasing everyone else in the cast and crew. Once the filming was called they aged twenty years and adopted serious expressions and repeated their lines and movements, often for several consecutive takes. The day was also interesting for our renewing our passing acquaintance with the author of the original story. She was on the set again today and in the afternoon took a break from sitting in on the production desk to appear as a hospital visitor. A combination of the heat in the room and tiredness had her asleep curled up on the end of my bed during a break in the filming. As I said later – we only met again yesterday and I did not expect to be sharing a bed … particularly as S. was in the bed next but one! The light was starting to fade outside so extra lighting was brought into the room raising the heat further. We were conscious of a need to get back to the house to pack and clear the house up for our winter absence. In the next break in filming we asked Zoe if there would be any more filming that evening and whether we would be needed for it. To our relief we were released with thanks, a recommendation to watch episode 15 or 16 to see ourselves and instructions to be sure to call into the company's office to provide our bank details for our fees! This was achieved along with a rapid house clear up and first stage of packing before we got back to town to enjoy our last evening meal out; an early one by greek standards at ten o'clock. The previous two days had been interesting and so typical of our new part-time life on the island where things "just happen" to you. Still it would make a good story to friends at home who normally ask us on our return —"so what have you been up to this time?

Elvis –

The original plans for the house had included a small "Juliet" style balcony on the front wall in front of the small pair of glass doors. As part of the drive to finish the house and attempt to stem the flow of money from our bank account to the architects a number of items were removed from the spec. The balcony was one of these. In our second year of actually living in the house we were still making amendments and improvements and we talked again about the balcony. As chance would have it we spotted another renovation project around the corner in the village where a small balcony had been added recently. The house wasn't finished or occupied and there didn't appear to be any current building activity so we wondered how we could contact the builders. Of course, the nearest kafenion would be the best bet and over a drink we made our enquiries. "Yes, it is Iannis, a local builder from town – a good man, an Albanian, he lives here with his family. I will tell him when I next see him ." As the days passed and our return to Sussex came nearer we concluded this would be something we had to leave until our next visit, no matter.

On the day of our flight with bags packed and the house cleaned and packed away we were minutes away from leaving when the doorbell rang. Outside we discovered Ageera from the kefenion standing with two smiling strangers who she quickly introduced before leaving for urgent business back at her kefenion. It was Iannis and his teenage son who quickly and confidently introduced himself – "I am Elvis and this is my father – we have come to discuss the building work. I will be able to translate." With that and for the first time I am able to say that Elvis entered the building!

I explained quickly that we would shortly need to go to the airport and that the work would need to wait until our next visit but we would like an opinion and a price quotation. We all went upstairs and I opened the small double doors to show them the space and we found the drawings on the plans that had been submitted for the building regulations. Iannis was quiet but business-like and after a quick diversion downstairs to look at the outside wall he returned and spoke in Albanian to Elvis – then alarmingly, prepared himself for our reaction to the translation by lighting a cigarette. The same thought went through our heads – we were shortly to lock up a house for several months – with wooden floorboards! Thinking quickly, I suggested we moved outside to admire the wall that the balcony would be fitted onto. Elvis translated that his father could provide a balcony similar to the one round the corner, fitted, painted for a price which is Dad wrote on a piece of paper and handed to us. The cigarette put out and we returned into the kitchen. We explained via Elvis that we would return later in the year that the price seemed agreeable and we would ring then to arrange the work. Phone numbers were exchanged, hands were shaken and with that Elvis left the building, with his Dad!

We checked the floorboards upstairs for glowing embers and reluctantly set off belatedly for the airport. We would return.

some of the illustrations in this book can be viewed in colour at https://www.pinterest.co.uk/geoffdendle/a-small-house-in-crete/